Moving With God

Past the Pain...

of divorce, death or any parting of lives once joined

A memoir of an extraordinary year in the life of
Pamela Woodbury Carlquist

Moving With God

Past the Pain...

of divorce, death or any parting of lives once joined

Pam Carlquist

A memoir of an extraordinary year in the life of
Pamela Woodbury Carlquist

Waggly Pup Press

2013 Waggly Pup Press, L.L.C.

Library of Congress Cataloging-in-Publication Data
Carlquist, Pamela
Moving With God Past the Pain...
of divorce death or any parting of lives once joined
ISBN 978-0-9883291-0-2

Printed in the United States of America

Book Cover by Kelli Ann Morgan of *inspire* Creative Services
www.inspirecreativeservices.com

Interior Book Design by Bob Houston eBook Formatting

For Mama and Daddy, who taught me how to love.
For John David and Will, who showed me how to laugh.
For Blume, Josh, Jess, Emmie Lou, Annie, Ebony and Zumi,
who personified how to live.

*"Why is it that when we talk to God,
we are said to be praying, but when
he talks to us, we're said to be schizophrenic?"*
— Lily Tomlin

Preface

It is early morning, still dark, the house silent and empty except for my teenage son, asleep in his bed downstairs. I have stolen from my own rumpled bed, creeping quietly down one set of stairs and up another to my study after another sleepless night, disturbed by dreams of all I have lost since John and I separated nine months ago.

How could I have let this happen, I ask myself for the hundredth time. How could I have thrown away 27 years, just like that? How could I?

I take a breath. It hurts to breathe. I breathe again. Regret consumes me. Anxiety. Sorrow.

Settling myself in a chair, I close my eyes, breathe again and pray.

The pain remains. I don't know what to do any more. Nothing helps.

Mechanically, I pick up a pen from my nearby desk, rummage through papers for a clean notebook and write. The writing comes easily. I don't think about it; I just let it go.

God,

Where are you? I need to talk to you. I need you to answer me somehow.

How can I go on with this life if you don't help me? I'm so alone and so empty inside. I keep reminding myself of what my meditation book <u>A Course in Miracles</u> says, that, "I am Spirit... safe and healed and whole." I don't feel healed, and I don't feel whole.

Since John moved out, I've felt lonely and incomplete and far less than perfect. Help me. I need you now more than I've ever needed you before...

Where are you, God? Answer me. You've answered so many others who say they're no more worthy than the rest of us, so why not me?

Please, please, talk to me.

Nothing happens, of course. What could? I close my eyes again, waiting for the heaviness to lift. I consider going back to bed and trying to sleep. In a few hours, my son Will will be up, and I'll have to smile at him and pretend everything is all right. He's so sensitive to my moods these days, so sad himself about the breakup. If I could sleep for even a few minutes...

But I don't sleep because suddenly I'm writing again. Only it doesn't feel as though I'm the one doing the writing. The words spill out upon the page.

Dear one, I am here, of course. Here, which is everywhere. I have always been and always will be. And so have you. You must know that only you can heal yourself, though in reality you are already healed. The symptoms may not reveal this yet, but trust that it is so. It has always been so. I can provide answers and guidance, but you must find this healing within yourself. Look for that which is divine and whole, that which is You. Open your heart, see the goodness in yourself right now, know that you are evolving on your journey to Me—and to You, the real You, the authentic You. See your Self as I see You—beautiful and warm and radiant.

Be still now as we talk together. Relax, breathe, be at peace. Let down your guard. Remember, defenselessness is a good quality; it is a quality belonging, as *A Course in Miracles* says, to the teachers of God. You may feel you have failed an important test today. You let a soul mate's—your husband's— anger ignite your own, which was lying like an ember waiting to flare to life. But really it was just a quiz and a small one at that. The ultimate test will end with the score of 'A.' Be assured of that. Use your time in this life to move in that direction, the direction of excellence and compassion and forgiveness. The most difficult task is to forgive and to love when you don't feel loved by another, especially by someone who has shared so much of your life with you and for whom you care so much.

Know that he is healing, too. His anger will diminish with time, and he will begin to see the blessings of your past and current relationship and your life together. Trust that all will work out as it should and that it will be beautiful, beyond anything you have yet known. Believe that. Believe. Have faith, my dearest one. You are safe with me. I love you too much to let anything truly dark befall you. All of this, even the breakup of your marriage, is for your healing and for the healing of many others. You have co-created it, each of you in your own way. Be patient. Meditate much. Pray much. See the beauty around and within you. Drink it in, and let it flow through your veins, cleansing and nourishing you.

All is well, my dear one, my love... All is well... All is well...

I stare at the page, the hairs on the back of my neck prickling. I read the words again and again, trying to grasp what is happening. At last, I reach for my pen, which has fallen to the floor, and answer.

I can't believe you're actually speaking to me, God, and actually writing through me. Is that who you are—God? Or are you a guide or an angel or something? I feel love and peace as I write this. Whoever you are, you must be very holy.

It is I. Don't you recognize me, Pam? Not that it matters so much. If I were a guide or an angel, I would still be God, speaking to you. They are all a part of me; you, all of you, are a part of me. So much a part that without even one of you, I would be incomplete. Yet God could never be incomplete, and neither could you.

You have questions for me. Concerns. Ask away.

Well... I have a lot of questions, mostly about my marriage and separation and the deaths of my loved ones and... all kinds of things. But before I get into that, I'd like to ask a different sort of question. As you know, I attended a workshop in Scottsdale last weekend. Right before it started, I asked you to help me decide on my next piece of writing. Should I revise my last book or leave it as is or start something new? I'm still not sure, and I do think it would help me to focus on something besides John, for a change.

Do whatever your heart tells you, Pam, with your writing and everything else—always. You get to choose. Remember, no choice is necessarily better or worse than any other, just different. One may seem to bring you more happiness, but the other may have important lessons for you to learn. You get to decide. That's just the way it is.

You did ask me to give you a 'sign,' and I obliged. You gave it to yourself really. Trust in that. You inadvertently left all three pieces behind at the hotel, didn't you? Now, that must tell you something, that you should begin a new draft or start a new book altogether. I suggest you start a new book. *Once, in the Meadows* was important for you to write; you had things to say, wounds to heal. It is a great work—or will be when you finally tackle it, when you're ready to write the final draft. But for now, begin anew, with a new spirit of adventure. I'll help you. We'll co-create this work together.

'Write your book. Write your book. Write your book,' I have whispered to you over and over. Trust Me. Trust your Self. Trust the Universe. And then just do it. You are Spirit, as are your brothers and your sisters, all of them. You have come to save the world, each in your own way. The Universe, which is God, is showing you how—literally.

Begin here. Begin now. Write your book, write your book, write your book...

Okay, I'm scared…

I don't know what to think about this. Could it be a trick of my brain just so I can pretend everything's going to be okay again? Or am I going crazy?

But that's stupid; I know I'm not crazy. I'm stressed and unhappy, yes, but not crazy—whatever 'crazy' is.

Is it possible… could it be… that maybe, just maybe, this is real, the answer to my prayers?

That's a novel idea.

Anyway I can try it for a while and see where it goes. And if I don't like it, I can just stop writing. I do feel better already, I have to admit, more hopeful, more ready to move on with life. And it does feel real to me, so I have to at least give it a try. I really would be crazy, when you think of it, to let an opportunity like this slip by without giving it a chance. Imagine, talking to God and having Him answer with real words!

And it does feel real to me… as I said before.

So…

…so, here goes, straight from the heart!

One

"Above all else, I want to see. Above all else, I want to see differently."
-A Course in Miracles

How does one begin? In the beginning, you say. "In the beginning, there was…." But what if I'm not sure how or when it all began, what then? *In medias res,* I tell my students, so I guess I should practice what I preach. *In medias res*—in the middle, of the mire and the muck and the pain.

These last nine months have been difficult, God, so difficult. This lifetime, in general, has been challenging—so many problems to overcome, so many obstacles to hurdle. But these last nine months, separated from my beloved, my husband, have been especially hard, harder even, I think, than when I was a teenager and lost both my parents. That was devastating; I felt alone and afraid. But it was a different kind of pain than the heartache I've felt since John left. My parents didn't really want to leave me, whereas my husband did. How do I cope with that?

Every day, I think, "How could you? How could you just

stop loving me? I thought we were committed to loving one another forever. How can you turn away so easily and move on to a different life? How can you do that to me—to our children, to yourself? Was I that bad?"

I guess the answer is, "Yes. You were that bad. I left, didn't I? And I haven't come back."

Help me with this, God. Give me some answers to these and other questions so I can understand, at last, and heal. So that others can, too, others who are going through these or other equally devastating challenges. Remind us that you're here with us. Help us understand; help us heal.

Of course, I'm here, Pam. I'm always here. And I will help you. But not in the way you think. Not by waving some magic wand and making it all feel better. Only you can do that—make it feel better, that is. And not through magic or whatever you think I use to create 'miracles.' I'll teach you to heal yourself and to find the answers you're seeking. I'll guide you and others to deal with the various challenges of life. But the fact is, you already have all the answers inside you. Everyone does. You have only to open your heart and find them.

Think about what you've just said. Think. Nine months. *Nine months.* It's significant that you waited nine months after your 'separation,' as you call it, to begin this correspondence. (In fact, you can never separate from anyone, certainly not your spiritual partner, with whom you've shared so much of your life, this life and others. Separation from any of your brothers and sisters is impossible, but we'll discuss that in more detail later on.)

Nine months. You needed just that amount of time for healing and for new ideas, many of which we'll discuss, to grow like an embryo inside you. And now the ideas are ready to be born, and you're ready to give birth, you who have become—have always been, though you have not been conscious of it until now— one with your authentic Self, your higher Voice, your God. One with Me.

"God's voice speaks to you all through the day," says *A Course in Miracles*. And I do. Thank you for finally listening.

I am listening, but I can hardly believe it. God Himself, speaking to me? It seems impossible, yet somehow I know it's true. You're you, and yet you're me, too, speaking in a voice that's wise and all knowing, yet that's both a part of me and far, far beyond me. It's an incredible feeling and yet so natural, impossible to describe. It's as though I've been preparing for this meeting with you all my life. All the reading and studying and meditating I've done all these years, and especially these last nine months—my retreat time, I've called it—have come together for just this moment.

It's amazing. Thank you.

Okay, now I'll shut up and listen. I just wanted to say thanks.

You're welcome. But actually it's not amazing, at all, Pam. What would be amazing is if I, your Father, your Mother, your Creator, your Lover, your Friend, your Soul, your All, *didn't* speak to you. I love you; I love all my children in a way that's beyond anything you can comprehend at this point. Throughout the history of the world, I have spoken to my children. Some have listened, and from them you have the great symphonies, the masterpieces, the songs and books and art that most touch your soul. Most people don't listen; most don't want to hear my voice. They've been taught to fear their god, who is angry and vengeful and thinks nothing of condemning them to an eternity of hell fire. How could such a god deign to speak to them?

And if he did, what then? How could they possibly keep an event of such magnitude to themselves? They would have to tell the world, their spouses, their children, their friends. And what would the world think if they said God spoke to them? Saints and 'sinners' alike have been burnt at the stake for less. At the very least, many would think them crazy.

Well, I have to admit that thought has occurred to me over the last few days since you first began speaking to me in this way. I do worry that if I tell people—my colleagues, my students, my friends, even my family—they'll think I'm a bit 'odd,' to say the least. It's hard to ignore that fact. To be perfectly honest—and I might as well be since I assume you know everything anyway—I've only told one or two people about this, and even then I've been pretty vague about it all. I've mentioned that I listen—notice I don't say 'talk'—to 'my higher voice' or 'my authentic Self.' Even the most spiritually advanced people I know seem to accept this explanation more readily than they would if I said I talked to God—*and* that he answered.

Yes, well, if it's of any consolation, you're not

alone in this, in your dialogue with me and in your reluctance to share that dialogue with others. I'm having these conversations with quite a few people these days, I'm happy to say. Some are writing them down, as you are. Others are using the ideas to teach workshops and classes or to paint works of art. Still others are simply listening and integrating my words into their everyday actions, nurturing the sick, healing relationships or just living lives that are more conscious and compassionate. They're changing the world in small, seemingly inconsequential, yet nonetheless momentous ways. Ask me questions. Talk to me, Pam. Then be still and know that I am God, a God who listens and loves and responds. If I can create a universe, for Heaven's sake, I can certainly talk to my creations. It's quite easy really. It's only hard if no one listens.

Good heavens—literally! I'm listening, God, and I don't care if people think I'm crazy. Or, at least, I think I don't. I certainly don't care enough to stop talking to you. We can figure out whether or not I should let others in on this later on.

Good, then let's get on with it. Let's go back to what we were talking about before, about your 'separation' from your husband. About any separation, yours or another's, whether it's the splitting up of a marriage or the death of a loved one or any other perceived 'loss.' For that's what this dialogue is all about, Pam—dealing with loss. Any loss. Any 'perceived' loss, that is, for there's no such thing as loss, in reality. I'll make that clear to you as we go. But let's look at the various problems in life, and you'll see that they appear to be problems because people see in them a kind of loss. Once you and others see these situations for what they really are, you'll realize that they're not problems, at all, but illusions, every one. And opportunities. When you recognize this wondrous fact, all problems will disappear from your life, evaporate, dissolve, as all figments of imagination inevitably do. When a child has a nightmare, she cries out in distress for help. But once she wakes up enough to realize that it was but a dream, she is at peace again, for she recognizes it for what it is, merely an illusion that cannot hurt her at all. So it is with all perceived problems in life.

With all due respect, God, that's easy for you to say. You see things more clearly than we do and have the vantage point of looking at all things with infinite wisdom. We, on the other hand, are limited in our perspectives. What might seem a mere scratch to You, Who knows how all things will turn out, can seem like a mortal wound to the rest of us who know nothing of the future. We move blindly through life, day after day and year after year, moment by moment. Naturally, we fear the unknown and hate our problems. Some of those problems result in separation and even death for us or for our loved ones. So what else could you expect?

Besides, what if that child's nightmare goes on and on, as in the concentration camps of World War II? As in the lives of those who have a terminal illness or who sit by the bedside of a loved one who's dying, yet can do nothing to help? As in the case of a painful separation or divorce? What about those? We're talking about tragedies and pain and heartache. How can you say there are no problems with all of those things going on all the time? They aren't illusions or figments of our imagination or nightmares from which we'll eventually awaken; they're real events. They're facts. Irrefutable facts. How can you possibly say there are no problems in life?

That's what this discussion is all about, Pam, helping you and others to understand. Helping you to see the perfection of the universe and of your lives. Helping you to remember who you are and who you want to be. And helping you to create the life that will allow you to manifest your most joyful and creative reality.

It's a lovely day outside. Let's take a walk together and begin. We have so much to discuss.

Two

"Be ye transformed by the renewing of your mind."
-Romans 12:2

As I'm sure you know, Pam, it's not what happens to you in life that's important so much as how you respond to the events in your life. You co-create every event, the happy, the tragic and everything in between. I'm using terms, by the way, that you can understand, terms such as 'separation,' 'tragic,' etc. In reality, separation does not exist, and there are no tragedies. You'll understand this when you recognize the perfection of the universe. I'll help you to more fully grasp this as we go along.

You co-created your marriage, and you co-created the joys you experienced during the 27 years of that marriage. However, you also co-created the less than happy times, the unloving and unloved times, even the 'separation' itself.

Wait a minute. I *allowed* the separation, but I didn't really want it. I wanted our marriage to work. John was the one who moved out. I just enabled him to do that because he seemed to want that and because I thought it was the right thing for both of us at the time. I assumed we'd keep working on our marriage; I even thought the separation would help us reevaluate and appreciate and eventually heal our marriage. John, on the other hand, started dating immediately; in fact, from what I've learned, I'm not sure he even waited until we were separated before he started seeing other women. He didn't try to reconcile, at all.

You wouldn't have allowed reconciliation even if he had wanted it, Pam. And if you had, you'd both have found yourselves back in a relationship that was only half working and, therefore, not working at all, not on the level each of your souls was seeking—that is, not on the level of true intimacy. For many years, you'd been leading lives of 'quiet desperation,' as one of your great teachers has put it. And so, John moved out, and you moved on. You mourned his leaving; you resisted it. You even begged him to come back at one point, if you'll recall. You felt abandoned and betrayed and very hurt. You felt you had failed at the one thing that mattered most to you—love. Despite all of this, you did move on. And when you did, you embarked on your greatest spiritual journey thus far.

Your greatest spiritual journey... Just think about that.

Yes, I suppose some of what you say is true. Okay, probably all of it is. I am grateful to John for moving out and for not coming back, even when I begged him to. I'm grateful, too, that I didn't just plunge right into another romance to ease the pain as I sometimes did, or tried to do, during my high school and college days, as so many people seem to do after a breakup. My goal, whenever I broke off a relationship in my younger days, was to jump right into another one as soon as I could. I can see now that that was a mistake. I didn't give myself time to really learn and grow, to be with myself and my sorrow and to see that I was fine, that I was enough just by myself. Instead, I looked for someone else to make me whole. And that expectation always resulted in disappointment because no one ever could complete me; only I can do that. I realize that now. The new relationship was often just a bandage, not a true healing or cure. Even my relationship with John was that, in a way. I always thought that, as my husband, he should be my other half, that he should fill all the voids. Of course, he never could; no one could.

Yes, you're beginning to see.

You're not the same as you were nine months ago, Pam; surely you must realize this. And aren't you glad? So much has happened since then, so many changes; and I'm not speaking of the events outside yourself to which you have responded, so much as the response itself. Just a few days ago in one of our first chats, you said that throughout your life, you've had to 'overcome' your problems. And you're right. Most of your life, that's precisely what you've tried to do— overcome each difficulty that has come along. That's the difference between the 'then' and the 'now.'

During these last nine months, you've stopped struggling to overcome—to swim upstream, to change the course of the tide—and have learned instead to surrender, to let life's circumstances take you where they will. You've stopped resisting, at least some of the time anyway, and have learned to float with the current, observing the ripples, the unexpected turns, the beauty of this new way. You've allowed the pain to come—invited it, breathed into it, faced your fears, and breathed out. And even when it seemed unbearable, you have told me—through tears, at times—that you were grateful for it all, for the lessons you've learned and the fears you've faced. Never once did you ask me to change it back to the way it used to be. Most people going through this kind of pain beg me to make the pain go away, to return their lives to the way they once were. You didn't. You weren't willing to settle for the mediocre any longer; you wanted more, for yourself and for John, for all creation.

"I accept this and anything else," you said, even in your darkest hours. "Anything, so long as I don't become bitter and angry and closed, so long as these experiences help to make me more loving and compassionate."

And they have.

Thank you for saying that, God. I do feel a change. I'm still unhappy at times, inconsolable, but I'm learning to go inside and talk to you about it and listen for answers. It has made all the difference.

Let's look some more at this 'separation' of yours, only let's not call it that anymore since, as I've said, there's no such thing as separation. You are a part of me your creator and a part of all creation always. As you are one with me, you are one with your brothers and sisters. You are like a wave in a vast ocean; as such, you contain all of the same qualities the ocean itself contains. You share these qualities with the other waves, with all creation. As long as you stay connected to your source, the ocean, you possess all the power you could ever want. However, if a wave were to separate from the ocean, it would lose that power, right? Isn't that what you would expect? You, the wave, would end up on the shore, disappearing into the sand perhaps or evaporating into the air?

But here's the great part that most people don't know. It's the reason you don't have to carry around the baggage of guilt and pain and sorrow, of regret or even anger for the things you've done or haven't done or for the things others have or haven't done to you. *You can never separate from me, your source, or from any of the other waves, your brothers and sisters who are also part of that source.*

You might think you're separate, at times, especially when you're feeling sad or hurt. Notice I did not say, "When you ARE sad or hurt." But, in reality, you are never separate. What you do or don't do to others, you do or don't do to me and to yourself; what others do or don't do to you, they do or don't do to me and to themselves, as well. We are one, eternally, lovingly, beautifully One. Always.

The doing and the don't-doing will never change that, nor will they make any part of creation any less divine or perfect than it was before. They might make you feel less happy for the moment, and that's important to notice so that you can act—so that you can do and don't do—in a way that brings peace and happiness to your heart. But they don't change who you are.

As water disappears into the sand or evaporates into the air, it just takes on another form for a while. Eventually, it returns to its source. Like the mists that rise into the air to become one with the clouds, like the rain that falls to the earth, like the water in the ground that ultimately finds its way back to the sea, so, too, will you return to me. And I will be waiting. In fact, you will never have left, for I am the ocean and the sand and the sky and all things in the universe that encompass everything else, even you. You are part of the beautiful whole, no matter what you do or don't do. So are your brothers—animals, plants, microorganisms, humankind, all of creation. Troubles, sadness, fears and anger—all are like a gray mist, like the darkness of night that temporarily hides the blue of the ocean from the eyes of the beholder. But even at night, the ocean is still there, as are the cliffs surrounding it and the waves crashing against the rocks and the sun that shines down upon it in the morning. As is all the Universe. Always there. Always perfect. Always One with Me—and You—We Who are Love.

Wow. I like that. It gives me hope. So you're saying that no matter what I do or don't do, you'll forgive me? That I'm connected to you always, even when I'm my most obnoxious or unlovable self? I like the idea of that.

On the other hand, I don't particularly like the idea of your forgiving John. I have to admit I'd prefer a vengeful, angry god who considers abandonment a sin and who will punish a husband for leaving his wife, or vice-versa, just because she (or he) is not as young and sexy as she once was, tossing her away as though she were nothing more than a piece of garbage and moving on without a backward glance. I think love is a decision, and I don't like the fact that John made the decision to love me and then changed his mind. I know it's a bit hypocritical of me to want you to forgive me and not John, but that's how I feel.

Perhaps you feel that way now, at this moment, but you don't usually feel that way. What are the words you pray almost daily? "For the continued healing of the hearts and marriage of John and me and for the reconciliation of our family as one, with John loving and forgiving me—and I, him—in a way that's beyond anything either of us has experienced or thought possible. And for love so beautiful, so pure and so true that it spills over into the world as we consciously use our lives and love to make a positive difference for all mankind and for all creation."

It's a lovely prayer, a prayer of forgiveness, an affirmation of what is and what can be.

Oh, yeah. I forgot.

It's a most blessed thing, forgiveness. As you forgive—that is, truly forgive, not just excuse a perceived offense but actually see beyond the gray mist of your prejudice to the perfect goodness that lies within, to that which IS—you will find a peace beyond anything you have yet known. And you will know, even in the darkest of times, that it was only your limited view, your lack of forgiveness, that kept you from noticing what was, is and has always been within others and yourself and, of course, John, all along.

Each of you may certainly make mistakes—that is, do or neglect to do something that causes hurt or anger in yourself or others—but one can never really sin. Even Judas himself did not sin; he only erred and then felt so remorseful that he took his own life, another error perhaps. Or perhaps it was what he felt he must do in that lifetime and in that moment. I do not judge him. The important thing is, there is no sin, only error; and if you insist upon using the term 'sin,' think of it only as not loving yourself, me and/or others enough.

Just as you would not punish your children for making a mistake—at least, I hope you wouldn't; you would instead teach them and help them to correct their errors—so I who am Love do not punish my children either. I send teachers and provide opportunities, which they may choose or not, to help them remember who they are. I'm happy for them when they feel happy and at peace—and even when they don't, for I know the time will come when they will. It *must* come. It's inevitable, for you are each one with me, God, and I am Happiness and Peace.

"In Him we live, and move, and have our being." -Acts 17:28. Say this often, and know that it is true, every word. And repeat, also, the verse to which you referred when you first wrote to me: "Spirit am I, a holy son of God, free from all limits, safe and healed and whole, free to forgive, and free to save the world."

-A Course in Miracles

As you heal—or rather, as you recognize your healing—you free yourself to save the world. Heal, Pam. Know that you are already healed and whole, even now.

All of that sounds good, intellectually; and I believe it, all of it. But it's hard to remember it when we see others and ourselves making mistake after mistake in our everyday lives. When we cut each other off in traffic or in a grocery line, when we yell at our children for messing up the house, when we curse our neighbors or colleagues if things don't go just right, when we compete for jobs or cars or houses or... The list goes on and on. Just living in this materialistic and very busy world makes it hard to remember we're one with our brothers and with you. Right now, for instance, I can't help but feel hurt and anger because of John's lack of love for me. It's hard to forgive.

When you feel this way because of John's—or anyone else's—actions, you're forgetting who you are and who you want to be. Who John is, too, which is Spirit. You're taking his actions personally, when in your heart you must know that what John does or doesn't do is about John, not about you. John has done what he must to heal, and so have you, who have helped to create this situation with him. Trust. Trust John, trust the Universe, trust your Self that all is working out perfectly.

As I said before, one of the most difficult things to do, but certainly the action of an evolved and enlightened being, is to return love for hate or indifference. For your own sake, try never to forget who you are and who you want to be. Would you allow anyone—any one individual—to rob you of this most precious gift of peace? I hope not.

Do you remember a women's retreat you attended several years ago when your children were small and you felt the need to get away from all of the mundane chores for a day? During one of the sessions, you drew a piece of paper from an envelope, and on it were the words, "Are you ready to be healed?" It was a message from me, Pam, in case you didn't know. As instructed, you closed your eyes and meditated on that question; and as you did, you heard the voice of your earthly father from long ago.

"Are you ready to be healed, Pamela?" he asked, and his face appeared before you. "Are you ready to be healed?"

"Yes," you answered, though you were a little frightened in saying yes. You weren't sure you were ready. You just knew you were tired of the pain inside, the doubts and fears, the gnawing sense of insufficiency that cropped up so often in your life, the feeling that things were not what they could be. You weren't quite ready to commit to healing at that time, but you took the first step. You said, "Yes." Every day since then, you have taken other steps. You have also stumbled, fallen, cursed the world and me, cried and clutched at the earth, refusing to move at times. And then you have picked yourself up and said, "Yes," again and taken another step. Now you're beginning to stride. You have been preparing for this day. The time for healing is now if you say it is.

Are you ready to be healed, Pam? Are you ready?

I... I think so... Yes. Yes, I am.

Then let's get on with it...

And I am ready...

...so ready to be healed. With all my heart, I want that. And yet...

There's this problem I have. It gets in the way of pretty much everything I do.

For example, when I first wrote my letter to God on that early winter morning, I didn't for a moment expect him to answer, not like this anyway. I never thought I could be a part of anything so wonderful. Not that I wouldn't have believed someone else who told me he or she was having an experience with God. I probably would have believed, depending on who the person was; I've always tried to be open-minded. But the truth is, I've never felt I was significant or worthy enough to have such an experience myself.

I'm extremely insecure, as you've probably guessed; I always have been. I'm hard on myself, too, constantly measuring and finding myself wanting. It's the pattern of my life, one I'd like to change.

"Then change it," you might say, and actually that's exactly the sort of thing I tell myself all the time. "Trust that this is happening, that God cares enough to speak to you just as he would to anyone else."

Intellectually, that makes perfect sense. Why not, I ask myself. And hope, like a timid, tired dove, stirs inside.

But then another voice, the small, cruel one that's also part of me, lashes out.

"You're not enough, Pam. You know that," it scoffs. "Not good enough, not pretty enough, not worthy enough, not athletic enough, not smart enough, not enough in any way. You make mistakes. You screw up. You go along just fine for a while, but then... same old, same old. Face it. You're just not enough, not now, not ever. God, talking to you? What a laugh!"

And all my self-loathing, all my uncertainty, like giant, gathering waves, come crashing down on me.

Are you ready to be healed, Pam? Are you ready?

I am. I just don't know how. Not yet anyway. But, oh, how I do want to learn!

Three

"In the stillness ask your True Self, 'Who am I?' Keep asking it until all false identity has dissolved and all that is left is the answer. It is an answer without end because you are infinite."
–Science of Mind   July 2001

This has been a time of great learning for you, Pam, for remembering who you are and what you have come to do. Be glad for this answer to your prayers, which you have co-created. Be glad you are learning to live your life more consciously.

You have begun to face your fears, and that's a healthy thing for if you don't face them now, you will have to—will choose to—later on. It's inevitable. If you have a wound, you eventually treat it so that the pain will finally stop. You might put off doing so, fearing the treatment more than you fear the injury itself. But ultimately, left untreated, the infection will become so acute that you will seek healing, even if the treatment is painful. So it is with life. If you have wounds to heal—if, for example, you have issues of low self-esteem or fears of abandonment, both of which you have experienced, by the way—you will co-create painful experience after painful experience until you're finally able to surrender, as you have done, until you can float with the current and become one with it, with your brothers and sisters and with Me, the Great Ocean. As you face rather than resist your fears, they will disintegrate like so much sludge sinking to the bottom of the sea and lying still or becoming one with the water itself. When fear ceases to scare you, it cannot stay for it is but an illusion, conjured by a tired mind.

Sometimes I want to say to you, God, "No more." Sometimes I'm tempted to say, "Put things back the way they were. They weren't perfect, but at least I didn't feel this pain." But I can't. I know that. And so I haven't because despite the pain, I've also felt an incredible sense of healing, even on the darkest days—or most of them anyway. A few times, I've even felt bliss, and those brief glimpses have helped me remember who I am and who I want to be. I believe I have a purpose to fulfill here in this lifetime; and I want desperately to fulfill it. I just wish I knew what it was.

What you're doing right now is part of it. Trust your heart and trust me. I am with you. I have been with you always.

Let's go back two years, to a day of blue skies and a sea that seemed to stretch forever as you sat on the lido in Venice, unaware of the strange event about to take place, an event that would change your life forever—the day you met Emma, the traveler, a messenger sent by me...

The woman Emma approaches you and your friends. She talks to you and offers you the 'gift of Spirit.' You sense immediately that she's different, that she has a mission to fulfill, that she's been sent to you for a reason. At first, you hold back, not sure whether to trust her or not. Does she want money, you wonder, or something else? But she asks for—and takes—nothing.

"You, my Self needs to talk to," she says when she spots you sitting quietly nearby listening to her conversation with the others. "You, my Self has come to visit." She speaks to you in a way that seems at once strange and yet oddly familiar. Then she asks you a most important question.

"If your Self could ask of Spirit anything that your heart desires, what would it be, Pam?"

You're taken aback.

"I've already asked Spirit," you say. "I don't know you. I don't feel comfortable telling a stranger something so personal."

Your friends depart, leaving the two of you alone together.

"Pam," she says. She looks you in the eye, and her voice is stern, unrelenting. "You do not know to whom you speak. I am a traveler. I have come from Spirit. I give you this opportunity today, an opportunity that many would wish for with all their heart. Will you let it pass you by, or will you take this gift? Now, my Self says to you again one last time,

'What do you ask of Spirit?'"

This time you don't hesitate. You tell her.

"I ask Him to renew a right spirit within me," you say. It's a pure request, you think, straight from the *Bible*—Psalm 51:10. It's a request you've made many times in prayer. It will bring you a nicer disposition, a lightness of heart, a bit more joy. More friends, you think. Better relationships. That's all.

But Emma is alarmed.

"You do not know what you are asking, Pam," she says. "You are not yet ready for this. You have a supportive husband, I think, a family, a comfortable home and all that you desire materially. Your request may require some changes in your life. What if you were to lose these things that you take for granted? How would you survive?"

"I've thought of that," you say, though you're not so sure now. You're worried that Emma may be right, that you're not fully aware of all you ask and all this may entail. You tell yourself you can make this request without sacrificing your marriage or the comforts of your home and of the world. Anyway, your marriage has already begun to unravel. It's fragile, at best. Tentative.

"This request may require more than you realize," Emma presses. "Think about it, Pam. Are you sure you want to make this wish?"

You think about your life, how dissatisfied you've been for years, how turbulent your thoughts, how self-deprecating and defeating, how unloving you've been to yourself and others, at times, unable to give love and unable to receive it as fully as you might.

"Yes," you say. "I'm sure. I ask God to renew a right spirit within me." And you mean it.

That was a momentous day.

Four

"Trust in the Lord with all thine heart; and lean not unto thine own understanding."
-Proverbs 3:5

Yes, I remember that day well.

In fact, I've never forgotten my conversation with Emma, though I did allow the memory to fade for a while. Several months after John left, I thought about it again and wondered if Emma's warning had come true, if this was the sacrifice I had to make to become the person I wanted to be.

I didn't require any sacrifice from you, Pam. I never demand or even want sacrifice from any of you. This was just the natural result of years of wanting more from life and from relationships than you were then experiencing and of seeking freedom from the many fears that you had not yet reconciled and that your soul was seeking to heal. One fear in particular that you've carried around with you since childhood—

before childhood, really—was the fear of abandonment. You were not only sad that your parents died when you were a teenager, you were angry with them for leaving you. In fact, you hated them for that. You were fearful that others you loved would eventually leave you, too.

No way! I never hated my parents; I loved them. I missed them. I wanted them to stay. You were the one who forced them to leave. They didn't want to get sick and die, so why would I be angry with them? With you, maybe, but never with them.

Think about what you're saying, Pam. Look into your heart. Do you really believe this? I think not.

You say your parents didn't want to leave you, yet I must remind you that no one leaves this earth without his or her consent. Your parents chose to die when they did long before they incarnated on this earth. They had many reasons for this. One of those reasons was for the healing they would offer you and your siblings. Each of you needed to experience this loss in order to heal wounds incurred in other lifetimes, long before this one.

Other lifetimes? What do you mean by that?

Does this come as a surprise, Pam?

Well... yes. As a matter of fact, it does.

No matter. It's not important. But you don't really believe I'd only give my children one chance to learn everything there is to learn and then throw them into the fires of hell if they didn't do things just the way I wanted them to, do you? That I'd offer them free will and then punish them because they took me up on my offer? What kind of an insane god is that? I have to laugh when I hear so many of the absurd ideas about me.

Or cry.

But getting back to your parents. As I was saying, no one leaves this world until he or she is ready. Nor does one choose to incarnate into this life unless the circumstances are such that they will help the soul to evolve, to remember who she really is. You co-created your life's circumstances. Your soul knew at a very early age that both your parents would die while you were still quite young. Don't you remember the many times, even before the age of ten, that you lay awake at night or awoke before dawn, brooding about their impending deaths? Once you woke your mother up early in the morning to comfort you; she was irritated at first, as you'll recall, but she soon saw that you were troubled.

"Don't ever leave me, Mama," you said amidst tears. She gave you a drink of water and ushered you back to bed, assuming you'd just had a bad dream.

You never told her about your fears; in fact, you never told anyone but me. I heard your cries, of course, Pam; but I certainly would not have changed that which you and your parents had chosen long before, which your souls had chosen, their early deaths in order that you and your siblings—and others— might confront your fears and heal.

I remember those times. Once when I was only a little girl, taking a bath, an overwhelming sadness welled up inside. I knew my parents were going to leave me soon, and I began to cry. Mama walked in, but I heard her coming just in time and ducked my face under the water to hide my tears. For some reason, I kept those feelings to myself, even back then.

I used to cry when she and my father would go out at night even when my grandmother, whom I adored, would tend me. My mother assumed it was because she had to leave me so often when I was young to help her sick father. But it was more than that.

> Yes, much more. You sensed even then that you had only a little time left with your parents in this lifetime, and you hungered to spend as much of that time with them as you could. Of course, when you became a teenager, you were less aware of this, assuming that since you'd already lost your father, you surely wouldn't lose your mother, too. You behaved much as any insecure teenager might behave, and I know you've deeply regretted your rebelliousness. I hope you'll at last forgive yourself, Pam; your mother forgave you long ago. In fact, she realized there was nothing to forgive for she knew you were merely a troubled young girl, acting out as many adolescents do.

I've always regretted that I was such a brat to Mama after Daddy died. I was so caught up in myself that I just wasn't there for her when she needed me most. Even when she was in the hospital, I was so mouthy at times. I've always wished I could go back and do things differently. Most people, as they grow older, can look back with their parents at the things they did or said as teenagers and laugh at them. I never got the chance to do that or to say I was sorry before Mama died. Even now, I can't help thinking this has been the biggest obstacle in my life, the thing that has kept me from loving myself and from feeling worthy of success and love from others. It's also the thing that has driven me to be an overachiever in so many ways, striving always to win this award or that or hear a word of praise here or there. I guess I thought if I earned enough awards or gained enough approval from others, I'd come to believe I was actually worth something. You ought to see my resume, God.

I've seen it. Pretty impressive.

Yeah, well, yours is probably a whole lot better! Anyway, as you know, the awards didn't work, and neither did the words of approval. When it came right down to it, I didn't believe any of it. I just figured I'd fooled the world somehow. I guess until I can forgive myself for the way I treated Mama and for so many other things, I'll never find peace.

Forgive yourself now, Pam. Now that you've become aware of this injury to yourself, correct it. Awareness is the first step, forgiveness the next, and finally healing and remembering who you are and who you want to be. Because that, of course, is what forgiveness is, as I've already stated and as I will undoubtedly repeat many more times until you fully get it. Forgiveness is seeing past the illusion of what *appears to be* to realizing what *is*, which is You, the perfect You that I created, that still is as it always was and always will be. You've made mistakes along the way, and you've learned from them. Learn now, and forgive yourself.

Practice the vow of *Ahimsa*, which is the practice of not causing pain through thought, word or deed; it's the key to complete happiness. But *Ahimsa* begins with self, Pam. Begin now. Love yourself. As you do, you will naturally love all others.

I'll try, God. I really will. You created me, after all. I guess I couldn't be too bad, right?

Not bad at all, Pam. Not bad at all.

Five

"The kingdom of God is within you."
-Luke 17:21

But let's talk more about the challenges of childhood, since this is an area upon which you and so many of your brothers and sisters dwell.

For many years now, you have considered yourself a victim, an orphan with a sad tale to tell. You've told others the story of your parents' early deaths, reveling in condolences and comments on your bravery, on the amazing ability of a child to move on as successfully as you have done. This role of victim has handicapped you in many ways, Pam. Lately, though, you've begun to move away from this limited view of yourself to a more enlightened one as you have come to realize that with this supposed childhood tragedy—and all of its subsequent challenges—came gifts, great gifts with opportunities for healing.

For you did indeed gain gifts from your parents,

their lives and their deaths, as they knew you would; as you knew, too, when you chose this life and when you chose your parents in this life. For one thing, you became much more self-sufficient as a result of their early deaths; for another, you took the blessings of life and of your loved ones less for granted.

Do you remember the afternoon, several months after your mother had died, as you stood in front of the big plate-glass window in your back yard, contemplating a Christmas without either of your parents? You looked into the glass and saw an image gazing back at you, the image of a skinny young girl of 14 with big frightened eyes and a sad face; and you made a vow to yourself, to that young girl, then and there, a vow you have never forgotten. You remember, don't you?

Yes, I remember. It's painful to remember.

"Some day," you whispered, "I'm going to have a family again—a beautiful, happy family. And I'm going to be happy again, as happy as I was when we were all together. I promise. Some day..." That's what you said, and that's what happened. You had that family, Pam; you fulfilled your promise to yourself.

Yes, for a while. But look at my family now, broken apart. Notice how I messed it all up again.

You've made some mistakes along the way, yes. You became rather controlling, for one thing, and that has hurt many of your relationships, certainly your marriage. But be gentle with yourself. It's understandable that you would want power over your life. Here you were, only a young girl; and suddenly you found your world topsy-turvy—your parents gone, your financial security ripped away and your heart broken. Naturally, you sought to gain more control in your life.

Furthermore, though you didn't realize it at the time, you allowed your fears to dictate your behaviors and to infect your relationships. You assumed that those you loved most would eventually leave you; your parents had, after all, so you decided others would, too. And you've helped them do just that—some of your friends, your boyfriends and later your husband. You were afraid to love too much, and you were afraid to let anyone get too close to you. "I must not be worthy of love," you assumed, "if even my parents couldn't love me enough to stay."

You've made mistakes in your life, as have others, and you've never forgiven yourself for them. Until you can forgive yourself, Pam, how can you possibly forgive others?

Your parents died, not because they didn't love you and your siblings enough to stay, but because they loved you so much that they chose before this lifetime to leave at an early age so that you might learn to live more fully while recognizing that you are enough in and of yourself, so that you might more readily confront your fears and heal and so that you might remember who you are and who you want to be—now, in this lifetime. While they were here with you, they did all they could to prepare you for your mission on earth. Then they left so that you—and others—might begin that mission.

And begin you did, kicking and screaming and resisting all the way. Resist no more, Pam.

Though your parents 'died,' they did not truly leave you. Surely you know that. Their souls are with you still; you and they are one. If only you had opened your heart more fully during times of need, you would have seen them beside you every moment. The accidents you have averted, the dangers you have fled. Angels watch over and protect you always, Pam. Over you and all others. You are never alone.

I want to believe that. Truly I do, but sometimes... sometimes I forget, I guess. Yet I have had experiences that were too incredible to be just coincidences. Several times, for example, I've felt that my children, off somewhere with their friends, were in danger. I've prayed for their safety and then later learned that they'd barely averted some accident. Other times, I've been guided to safety myself. Once while I was speeding home from college during a Thanksgiving break, I unexpectedly felt a strong urge to pull over.

"Slow down," a voice inside my brain screamed. "Slow down NOW!"

It was so compelling I didn't even stop to question it. I glanced in the rearview mirror, moved into the right-hand lane, braked and coasted to a crawl, all within a minute or less. The next thing I knew, my rear tire blew. At the rate I'd been driving, I'd probably have died; and since the highway was full of traffic that day, I'd very likely have taken others with me. Thank you for your warning.

So often I've felt your protection and known you've heard my prayers. I remember once in particular when, as a young girl, I made a most unusual request of you—to see my dead mother again, an appeal, amazingly, that you answered.

Yes, of course. I remember it well.

Six

"The things which are impossible with men are possible with God."
-Luke 18:27

It was back in 1963, when I was 14. Daddy had died two years before of cancer and Mama, just a few months earlier of what I always believed was a broken heart. I thought my world had come to an end.

It was almost Christmas, as I recall.

Yes, Christmas, and yet nothing—not the carolers, the tree, even the gifts—could stir any excitement in me. They were just reminders of what had been and what would never be again.

One afternoon, as the wind whipped about me and the rain fell, I trudged home from school to an empty house. I still remember how I felt as I stood outside, cold and wet but hating to go in. Finally I stumbled out into the back yard, dropped to my knees and begged you to help me. I cried and cried, something I hadn't let myself do since Mama died. And I prayed.

"God," I said. "I don't want to go on like this anymore. Please, please change everything back to the way it used to be."

Yes, I remember. You were so sad.

I knew it was impossible, the thing I was asking for, but I asked anyway. "At least, let me see her one more time, God. Let me say good-bye—for Christmas."

Your prayer touched me, Pam, for it was the prayer of a child, a pure prayer that came straight from the heart.

Well, you took your time about answering it, I must say, God. Days slipped by, then weeks, and I forgot all about my prayer. Christmas came without a single sign of a miracle. I celebrated with the family, smiling, laughing, pretending to be happy for their sakes—and they, I'm sure, for mine. I went to bed early that night, exhausted, tired of the pretense and of the dreariness of my days.

But that night I dreamt of Mama in one of only two color dreams I've ever had. She came to me in our rose garden, gathered me close to her and said good-bye. I felt the warmth of her body next to mine and smelled the fragrance of roses in her hair. She told me she loved me, would always love me and would always be nearby. I had only to open my heart to her, she said, and I would know that she was there.

When I awoke, she was gone. But the smell of roses lingered in my room, and I felt her presence for a long time afterward. I have only to remember my dream to feel her now.

Thank you, God, for this great gift. It was the best Christmas present ever.

You're welcome, my dear.

But will you tell me this? Was it real, or was it just a dream? I mean it seemed real, but... Well, was it?

Of course, it was real, Pam. Your dreams are but reflections of reality. You asked for your mother, and you allowed yourself to receive her. Why wouldn't she come to you, her youngest child, who needed her as you did then? Do you think a little thing like death could separate those who truly love one another? Never, not for an instant. You called, and she came. She took you into her arms, held you close and told you she loved you, would always love you, loves you still. As your love for her grows, so does your love for others. All others. Inclusive love. Unconditional love. Eternal love.

That's what you learned from her and what you can pass on. Will you do it? After all, you've asked to be one of my teachers. Then be one. "To have love, love and be loved," your wise Benjamin Franklin said. "To have peace, teach peace that you may learn it... To have all, give all to all." So says *A Course in Miracles*, and so say I.

And so said your mother in her own way that early morning long ago, that moment, which is yesterday, today and tomorrow, which is now and which is forever... and ever. Amen.

Seven

"I believe I am always divinely guided. I believe I will always be led to take the right turn in the road. I believe that God will always make a way where there is no way."
-The Power of Positive Thinking by Norman Vincent Peale

God, I keep wondering about something. Are the words in this book really yours? Or is my mind just making this whole thing up to suit my needs? I don't want to do that. I want this to be a pure source for your truths.

Then let me speak. Don't revise my words. Leave my part to me. You're so worried about organization and grammar and all the little mechanics of putting this together. I'll help you. Trust me. I created the world, didn't I? Let me write this without interference.

Should I start all over? Have I changed the things you said?

No, of course not. My message has remained intact despite your attempts at times to meddle. Don't try to manipulate my words, Pam. Just listen and write. You'll find a pure and untainted message. I've been helping you; most of your revisions have had to do with your questions and not my answers. But I do feel that you're trying to take control. It's a problem you have, remember?

I'm trying not to do that anymore. I'm trying to give up control and surrender completely.

Are you? Truly?

Yes.

Then do so now. Let go and let God. Literally. You'll be glad you did.

I will. I promise. And when this book is finished, I think your name and not mine should appear on the cover. I'm just a filter for this.

I wouldn't say you're a filter but rather the vessel through which my words pass. Think of it in this way, Pam. As your veins and arteries are the channels through which your blood transfers to all parts of your body, so you become the duct and I the life-blood that courses through you and that infuses your voice with words and ideas for the book. However, as I pass through you, your cells inevitably join with mine, and your words become part of the song. So, though I send these thoughts to the world through you, I bring your essence with me.

Yes, I am the author of this book, but so are you and so are all your brothers and sisters who have in even the most minute ways affected you and the very thoughts you've set down in writing.

These ideas may seem foreign at first to some who will read them, as they have to you at times. But have no fear. Many will remember an ancient song, a chord here, a verse there, a symphony, a chorus; and they will come home.

Open your heart, and I'll pour forth words of invitation and song. They'll pass through you and through all who read them, and you shall never, ever be the same.

He's right, of course...

I have been a control freak all my life. I'm trying to do better, but I still have a long way to go...

And yet...

...And yet (damn it!), I've come a long way, too, a good long way; I've made progress in this area and in many others. And I think it's time I acknowledged that part of myself, the part that tries to do the right thing, instead of dwelling on my 'faults' all the time. Time I started celebrating what's right about my life, instead of struggling to manipulate or change it into something different, something 'better.' Isn't that what happiness is, after all? Loving, enjoying what IS? Isn't that what God's been trying to say? (Or maybe 'trying' isn't exactly a God-verb.) And isn't it time I listened!

And He's right about my role as victim. For much of my adult life, I've let my orphan status become my identity, which is a pretty silly thing considering my parents died 40-plus years ago and here I am in my 50s still carrying that role around. I've allowed my perceptions of this to diminish my happiness and my relationships, even—especially—my relationship with myself.

And something else, something that just came to me a few minutes ago, something that makes all those years of self-pity seem even more ridiculous: Given the chance to decide all over again (in that Pre-Life or whenever it was I supposedly decided all of this), I wouldn't trade the 12 and 14 years with my father and mother for 100 years with any other parent. Not for a single moment! They were part of my destiny. Their lives and their deaths brought me to where I am right now—sad and separated from my husband, yes, but also blessed as the mother of two wonderful sons, the sister of three incredible siblings, the teacher of thousands of amazing students and the friend of so many wonderful human beings (and fuzzy, furry ones, too). A person who has experienced extraordinary life adventures, warm and wonderful times, infinite abundance... and now, a woman who has spoken to, and heard from, God Himself!

Amazing!

I don't know how I'll feel in 10 minutes or 10 hours or 10 days, but right now I feel nothing but gratitude. And right now, I'm so thankful for everything, even my separation from John. Surely some good shall come of it.

To God and to the Universe, to all of Life, I give thanks. To all that has been and to all that will ever be—past, present and future—I say YES!

Yes! Yes! Thanks! And Yes!

Eight

"Ask, and it shall be given you; seek, and ye shall find; knock, and it shall be opened unto you."
–Matthew 7:7

Good morning, God. Another day. It's been a while since we talked like this, and I'm longing to hear your voice. Once again, I promise not to 'meddle' or 'manipulate' your words, ever. I'm open to whatever you have to say. Will you speak to me today?

Of course, I will—to you and to all. I've been waiting for this time with you. Eternally, patiently, eagerly waiting. And now, this eternal Now, here you are asking and receiving, seeking and finding, knocking and watching the door open wide, ever wider, before you, at last, inevitably and forevermore.

You've had much on your mind lately. Let's talk.

Thank you, God. It hardly seems fair for me to expect you to make time for me, when I've made so little time for you lately.

Yet here you are, always here for me whenever I call.

> And even when you don't, consciously anyway. In
> fact, your soul calls to me always, every moment—and
> mine to you and to all beings, all Creation.

I'm sorry I've been so distant lately, especially over the last three weeks. This first holiday season away from John has been especially hard—not that I've been away actually, which is part of the problem. We've spent so much time together doing family things for the boys' sake that I'm reminded all the time of what's changed in our lives.

The worst part is I've been so busy I haven't made time for you, which is crazy because I've needed to talk to you more than ever.

> Your heart is aching, my child. I can see that.
> You want your marriage and family back as they once
> were. And yet, trust, believe, love. All will turn out as
> it should. Or don't trust. Don't believe. Don't love.
> And it will still work out, though it may take a bit
> longer.
>
> What are you yearning to ask of me now, Pam?
> By the way, you don't have to include these personal
> chats if you eventually decide to publish this. Pick and
> choose later on, if you wish. Only speak to me with
> your heart now. Don't wait.

Is John coming back, God? Can he ever love me again? He seems so happy to keep things as they are. He rationalizes that the kids are "better than ever." He doesn't seem inclined to change anything. I miss him so much. Can you help me stop loving him? Stop asking for him? How can I ever love anyone else if I hold onto him?

Ah, there you have it: Stop holding on. Let go, Pam. Remember that even as I, God, choose the highest good for you, even more I choose your will for you—your will and everyone else's, too, not mine, though truly they're one and the same. The surest measure of love comes from allowing another the freedom to choose his or her perfect will. That's why you must choose John's will and let him go. Send him on his way. No, more. BLESS him on his way.

Can John ever love you again, you ask. Yes, of course. But perhaps not for a long time and perhaps not in exactly the way you wish. Will John come back? Yes, in time, if he chooses to come back—and if you, at that point, choose, as well. And no matter what may happen, the future will have been worth all the heartache that each of you has endured. John will have found love in his heart for himself and for others, for me and for you, too. His will be a love that has known pain and has learned about loss but about healing, too. He—and you—will be ready to love in a way you've each only dreamt of, up until now.

Open yourself from this moment forward to loving all. Don't wait, and don't limit yourself to John. Open your heart to all creation. As you learn to be warm and affectionate, you'll laugh again. And when you can laugh enough, truly laugh, you'll draw John—and others—to you. He'll remember an ancient love, bathed in forgiveness, sweetness and light.

Yes, John will come back—in whatever way he

chooses—when you have learned to laugh again. Ironically, when that happens, it won't really matter anymore one way or another, for you will have found joy unspeakable with or without John. You're finding it already. Let the child within you out. Laugh out loud. Take life, and yourself, a little less seriously. Lighten up. When you were a child, you were so lighthearted at times. You loved to laugh and to make others laugh. You've allowed the somberness of life weigh you down. Let your real Self come through. Laugh, my child. Love and laugh. The world awaits your joy.

I want to lighten up, to laugh at all of life's troubles, but sometimes it's easier said than done, God.

Yes, you feel broken, and you're not alone in this. Take this message to a broken world. The world is filled with thoughts of separation and loneliness. And yet, that's not the way I wanted it or want it now. In truth, it's not the way it is. There is a world beyond this world, and it's here right now. Only open your heart, and you'll find it. When you do, you'll see that it has been here all along.

Love. Laugh. Live joyfully and fully!

I am with you always.

Nine

"When I am healed, I am not healed alone."
-A Course in Miracles

Thanks for your help yesterday, God. I'm feeling a little better. But if it's okay, I'd like to change the subject for a while. Could we talk about something else today?

Of course, whatever you'd like.

I'm not finished with the topic of marriage-gone-awry, mind you. Heaven forbid! I've got tons more whining to do on that subject!

Ha! I'm glad to see you can joke about it, Pam.

As for the 'heaven forbid' part, though, I plead innocent. Your species can engage in that sort of activity any time you like, provided you leave me—and heaven—out of it. Or not, I suppose. Free will is free will.

But we can discuss 'forbidding' and 'judging' and all the other crimes of which I'm charged another time. For now, let's walk together and talk about other things. You have something on your mind, I think. What is it?

I have some questions about a student I once taught and others who are in the same position she was in. I've often thought of her and wondered what her life is like now, after everything she went through as a child.

I used to think it odd that relatives or close friends could ever become so estranged they'd part ways forever. One would think they'd put aside their differences and reconcile if only for a little peace of mind. But when I consider Amy and others like her, I realize how complicated relationships can be and see that 'separation' (sorry—I know you'd prefer another word, but I can't come up with a better one at the moment) is sometimes the only reasonable alternative for those involved.

May I ask you about her, about Amy, and about so many others in this world?

Ask away, Pam. It's why I'm here.

Okay. Well, time flies; and it's probably been 20 years or more since I first saw Amy. She was a skinny little girl of 12 when she walked into my 7th grade classroom that first day of school. Little did I know then that she'd been the victim of an incestuous relationship with her father since she was three. She hated it, of course, but assumed her life was like every other girl's—until third grade, that is, when during a sex education workshop she learned otherwise. Immediately she went to her teacher for help. For a few months, she lived with a foster family while her father attended a rehabilitation program, and then the state returned her to her home. Again and again, the cycle continued: Her father abused her, she reported it to authorities, she was assigned to a new foster family, her father enrolled in the requisite rehab program and the state sent her home again. By the time she was in my class, she'd lived with many different families but particularly loved the one she was with at the time.

"It feels so good to go to bed at night and know I can just sleep," she told her counselor, who passed this information on to me.

Within a few months, the state intervened and sent her home again.

As you know, Amy's story is anything but unique, God. Every day, men, women and children are victims of rape, incest and violence of the most barbaric sort; one has only to open a newspaper to see this. Most are innocent victims, and so many lead dysfunctional lives as a result of the abuse, lives steeped in fear, distrust and even guilt forever afterwards. They're afraid much of the time, and many of them question themselves their whole lives, wondering if they might have resisted more, if they might have done something to stop the father or brother or stranger who perpetrated these crimes against them.

I know you've given us free will, God; and I assume that's why you don't prevent—or forbid—these things from happening. But surely you have some words of comfort for the victims and some insights and clarity for all of us. Could you help us with this please?

Yes, but first, Pam, you must realize that each is a victim in his or her own way—the perpetrator, as you put it, and the person upon whom these acts of violence are committed. The biggest challenge in all of life's problems, certainly in the cases of rape and incest and all acts of outrage, is to stop seeing oneself as the victim and to become instead the victor, to cease blaming oneself and, also, to rise above any seeming injustice and injury from another. Though it's not as apparent, the perpetrator not only injures another but wounds himself or herself, as well. Giving and receiving are one, in truth. What you confer on another, you confer equally on yourself; and what others bestow upon you, they bestow upon themselves, as well.

But in every circumstance, one can decide what gifts to keep—the gift of pain or the gift of forgiveness, the gift of hatred or the gift of peace. One can use each experience, even the most brutal, to become more present, more compassionate, even perhaps to educate society and help other 'victims.' Or that person can shrivel up inside, fearful and unwilling to live beyond the veil of victimization. Each experience has the capacity for healing; each holds the choice of heaven or hell.

Oh, wait. That reminds me of a story I once heard. Want to hear it?

Go ahead.

I hope I can remember it correctly. I think it goes like this: According to a legend, as the Buddha wandered from town to town, performing acts of kindness, many people hurled insults and even stones at him. Even so, he responded to all with love. One day one of his disciples, observing this, exclaimed in frustration, "Master, why do you allow people to mistreat you this way? Every day you go from village to village, showing nothing but compassion to all. But still the people abuse you. The next time someone throws a rock at you, pick it up and throw it back. That way, the villagers will think twice before hurting you again." But the Buddha only smiled and answered his disciple with this question: "When someone offers you a gift and you refuse to take the gift, to whom does the gift belong?"

I guess he was saying pretty much what you're saying now, that when someone hurts you, you can choose what gifts to keep—gifts of hatred and vengeance or gifts of forgiveness and love. Right? And the giver inherits the rest.

Exactly. A person, especially a child but many others, as well, may not be able to avoid the abuse (though I tell you again, each of you co-created the circumstances of your life when you chose to come to earth, and you continue to co-create them each and every moment). Nevertheless, that person, especially as she grows older, can decide which ancillary gifts to keep and which to give back to the world—IF she can first become aware of this possibility of choice and IF she can look the abuse in the face without resistance, confronting her fears and realizing she has survived them and will survive all future events, even death, since the soul lives on. Only then will she become fearless or, at the very least, able to manage her fears. She can decide to forgive her abusers, forgive herself and, where possible, remove herself from future abuse. At the very least, she can choose the "last of the human freedoms," as my son and your brother Victor Frankl, a Holocaust survivor, phrased it. This freedom

is the choice to respond to hatred with love, the choice
to forgive, the choice to heal. As one person heals, so
does the world, for you—we—are one. I do not say
this is easy, yet it is inevitable when one fully and
finally immerses himself in life, every moment of life,
without resistance, when one sees that each moment is
an opportunity for healing—healing oneself, others,
the world.

That's hard to do—forget the injuries and pain, especially
that kind of pain, and just move on.

And yet that is what one must do. One must
forgive oneself and one's supposed enemies. A child
who is the victim of sexual abuse from his brother or
father or mother may actually give into the incestuous
relationship in order to survive, may even think he or
she enjoys it for a while. Later, looking back, that
person will often feel not only violated by another but
by himself and will wish with all his heart that he had
struggled more, had fought back. She, he, they were
only children; and even if they were adults, so many
factors come into play here. One is naturally loyal to
and compassionate for one's own family members.
One sees beyond the action to the frailty of the other
person. It's natural that a child will give in, sometimes
willingly, to the sexual exploitation by a family
member because that child innately wants to be loyal
and to make that person happy. Later, the child may
only remember that he went along with what he now
perceives as a perverse act, and he will blame himself
as much as he blames the perpetrator. She will see

herself as vile and contaminated and unworthy of true love from a spouse or significant other and will do whatever it takes to prove to herself, her partner and the world that what she believes about herself is true.

Yet she must forgive if she wants to be happy; it's the only way. She must love herself and others, even her perpetrator, despite the defects. Only then can she free herself and free the world. It's important.

Hear me, My Children. Forgive yourself in all things—ALL things—and help the world, all others, to forgive themselves, as well. Cease to be the victim in every way, and you will find that you are indeed the victor.

Love and laugh, no matter what has happened to you in the past. The past is over if you but choose to let it go. Live now. Send the energy of forgiveness out into the world, a world that is longing to heal. Yes, love and laugh. The world will laugh with you. And so will I.

Ten

Hi, God. Today I received this e-mail:

God Speaking

A man whispered, "God, speak to me."
And a meadowlark sang. But the man did not hear.
So the man yelled, "God, speak to me."
And the thunder and lightning rolled across the sky. But the man
*   did not listen.*
The man looked around and said, "God, let me see you."
And a star shined brightly. But the man did not see.
And the man shouted, "God, show me a miracle."
And a life was born. But the man did not notice.
So, the man cried out in despair, "Touch me, God, and let me
*   know you are here."*
Whereupon, God reached down and touched the man.
But the man brushed the butterfly away and walked on.

I like this. It reminds me of all the ways you speak to us, even when we don't actually hear your voice. I hope the time comes when we will see you in everything.

I hope so, too, Pam, for on that day you will have remembered who you are. And you will never, ever forget.

Eleven

"Be patient with all that is unsolved in your heart and try to love the questions themselves like locked rooms and like books that are written in a very foreign tongue. Do not seek the answers, which cannot be given you because you would not be able to live them. And the point is to live everything. Live the questions now. Perhaps you will then gradually, without noticing it, live along, some distant day, into the answers."
-Letters to a Young Poet by Rainier Marie Rilke

I'd like to ask you about something else now—about death, the death of any loved one but, in particular, the death of one's child. Very soon I'd like to talk to you about the death of one's partner or spouse. Many of my friends have experienced this, as did my mother and quite a few others I've known. It must be so difficult!

But for now, if you don't mind, let's talk about the loss of one's child. One of my cousins, for example, lost both of her children when they were very young. One daughter had health problems from the time she was born; but after months of complications, the doctors discovered the problem and operated.

The little girl blossomed. She began gaining weight and laughing and playing just as any normal child would do. Then, just when Deb and her husband thought they could relax and enjoy this baby, she developed a blood clot that went to her brain and remained in a coma for eight years until she finally died.

My cousin showed amazing courage throughout the ordeal. But as if this tragedy weren't enough, her husband fell in love with one of the nurses taking care of their daughter, and eventually the two divorced. Soon afterwards, she and her older daughter moved to another town and tried to get on with their lives. However, at the tender age of 16, this daughter died in a car accident, leaving her mother all alone. Along the way, she lost her father and brother and eventually her mother, too.

My cousin is just one of many who have had way more than their share of tragedies during their lifetimes. Why is that, and what would you say to these people to help them cope with such insurmountable odds? It doesn't seem fair.

And yet it is fair, Pam, for these tragedies, as you call them and as they must seem to be, are filled with gifts, as well. Yes, your cousin lost her youngest daughter—first to poor health brought on by a birth defect, then to a coma, then to death. She lost her husband to an affair and her older child to death, too. So many times she cried out to me to help her. So many times she asked me why these things were happening to her. The answer is this: She invited these tragedies when she accepted this life, long before coming here. She had issues she wanted to deal with in this lifetime; she had fears she wanted to face and move past, for once and for all. Her children also chose their lives, their parents, their destiny and,

ultimately, their deaths. They willingly relinquished
their earthly lives at an early age in order to help your
cousin and others heal and evolve in the way they
needed to. They are soul mates with their mother and
can never really leave her, for their hearts are entwined
forever. All whom you love become a part of you
forever; indeed, as you are one with me, you are one
with all always.

Don't you see the connection of this to all else,
Pam, to your questions concerning your 'separation'
from your husband and your queries about victims of
rape and incest and violence? To all of the questions
you have asked in the past, to those you are asking
now and to all you will ask in the future? The
questions are important; you must ask them, of course.
The answers will differ to a point, but they'll remain
the same, too, for they're eternal, unchanging and,
above all, true. You see in all of these problems loss.
You feel each supposed tragedy somehow takes away
from the people involved—their happiness, their
abundance, their love, their joy, their loved ones, etc.
etc. But 'loss' and 'separation' do not exist; only love
does. The answer to all your queries, then, is this:
Only love remains.

Even so, continue to ask the questions, of
yourself, of all others and of me. Live the questions
until you understand them, and live the answers that
come. Live everything, even the supposed tragedies.
Live all without resistance, for only then will you find
that in the midst of sadness comes joy, in every
shadow appears sunshine and in every birth pain is a
child waiting to be born.

Twelve

"Peace I leave with you, My peace I give unto you: not as the world giveth, give I unto you. Let not your heart be troubled, neither let it be afraid."
-John 14:27

God, why is there so much violence in the world? Wars and fighting and terrorists are everywhere, even here at home on our own soil. Planes, shops, schools, theaters, even churches have become targets for completely random and irrational acts of murder. It makes me sad to see the world so full of fear.

Yes, but recognize that the terrorists of the world mirror the terrorist within each of you, Pam. And remember that you, too, at times, base your life on fear. The first place to begin, if you want to eradicate violence, is within yourself. Fear often begins with a small event and then magnifies into something much bigger.

Let me show you an example. Do you remember

when you were 13 and invited to your first teenage party?

Well, yes, I think so. But I don't see...

Wait. You will. If you'll recall, only the most 'elite' students in your class were invited; and you—skinny, awkward little Pam Woodbury—was one of them. Never mind that it was only because you'd been hanging out with some of the more popular girls on your church softball team and that the boy giving the party, seeing you with them, had assumed you were 'one of the gang.'

Whoa! Wait a minute. Did you—God, Creator of All—just say, "skinny, awkward little..."

I was reflecting YOUR thoughts about yourself, Pam, and maybe the thoughts of a few others, as well, but...

Okay, okay, let's get on with this, shall we?

I was going to add that if others thought that, they were blind, as were you. Truly. You were—and all of my creations always are—beautiful, through and through. Some of you just have a hard time recognizing that in yourselves and in others at times.

Anyway, getting back to that night, you went to the party, excited, elated and happy, only to find that the most handsome boy there, the one you particularly liked...

Jim.

Yes, Jim... had singled you out to the others as a 'skag,' thus one to be avoided at all costs. Once he made the pronouncement in a whisper loud enough for all, including you, to hear, he sealed your fate. Or perhaps you sealed your own.

Me? I sat there dying inside.

True, though you had—you *always* have—choices, even if they're a bit difficult at times. Anyway, the boys in the rather unkind fashion of young men that age took turns dancing with you but made it very obvious that it was the last thing they wanted to do. You were humiliated. Then came the spin-the-bottle game; and, of course, the bottle inevitably turned toward you. The boy who spun it was anything but gracious about kissing you. You wished you could curl up in a corner and disappear.

Yes, I did. I couldn't wait to get out of there. But you're right; I did have a choice, though at the time I was so shy I didn't realize it. If only I'd had the courage to get up early on, thank my host and leave, I could have saved myself some embarrassment—and dignity! But, of course, I couldn't—or didn't anyway. I wish I had.

You were young and timid and knew little about cruelty and the ways to deflect it, so it was understandable that you sat there smiling and pretending, trying to be gracious, all the while praying for the party to end. And end, it did—for the others, that is. Unfortunately, the party didn't ever end for you, for you believed that what Jim said was true. You were a 'skag,' unfit for human company; it's what you were then, you thought, and what you would forever be. Jim—someone important—had said so. And you believed it, as have so many others who have believed what a friend or a partner or a parent or someone else has said about them in words or in other ways. Despite the dances you later attended, the titles you won, the hearts you broke (even Jim's), you held onto the belief that you were somehow less than everyone else. You allowed that belief to infect your life and your relationships.

You and so many others in the world—the terrorists and the victims—have allowed the past to rule the present.

You're saying I've been the terrorist of my own life.

Yes, you have. Many times. Let the party end now. It has gone on too long. Pray that you and others will wage war on fear—all fear—and conquer. Practice. Recognize it the moment it creeps into your mind, whether it's the fear of death, a terrorist act or merely a moment of self-doubt that comes over you when things don't go quite as you wish, when someone says or does something that hurts you. Refuse to allow feelings of resentment or hurt or anger to linger for even a moment. See all such feelings as fear. Look them in the eye, size them up, analyze them and try to understand their root, which always lies within you. Then replace those feelings with love—unconditional, nonjudgmental love—for others and for your Self.

As for the terrorists of the world, pray for them that they might transform their own fears—their hatred and bitterness, their misunderstandings and prejudice, their past and all of their misconceptions about it—with peace and love. As we've already discussed, it's not so important what happens to you in life as it is how each of you responds. Answer all events, even those from your past, with love. Find the gift of that night so long ago; it has allowed you to be who you are today. You are a woman of light and love; you are compassionate and beautiful. More and more often, you are able to see the compassion and beauty in all others. Help them, all of them, to see it in themselves.

Those who directly or indirectly have been 'victims' of 'terrorists' are either gone from this earthly life and, therefore, at peace; or they remain and have chosen whether or not to continue to be victims or whether to use the opportunity to evolve spiritually, emotionally and in every other way. They can say, "Poor me," or they can use their newfound strength to turn their trials into triumph.

Yes, pray for the terrorists of the world and for the terrorist within. Let no fear remain. Be fully present in every moment. See the good in every event, the gift in every supposed tragedy and the opportunity in every instant. As you do, you'll see that you have nothing to fear, ever. You'll raise your energy levels to love, joy, peace, even enlightenment in this lifetime; and you'll learn to fully live.

How beautiful that will be. Peace to you and to the terrorist, within and without. Peace to all of you, my beloved children. Peace.

Hmm. A terrorist...

I've never thought of myself as a terrorist before, and I don't much like it.

But I guess I do understand what he's trying to say. I have been my own worst enemy at times, and I am extremely judgmental. I critique just about everything I think, say and do and everything everyone else around me does, too, though I'm usually much kinder about other people than I am about myself. I also evaluate every event that occurs—'This is good,' 'This is bad.'

None of it makes me particularly happy, mind you, yet it's become such a habit that I have to catch myself in the act in order to stop myself—'to know, shape and free the mind,' as Jon Kabot-Zinn puts it.

I've memorized this quote from *A Course in Miracles:* "Judgment and love are opposites; from one come all the sorrows of the world, and from the other comes the peace of God Himself." I think it pretty much sums up the way I feel whenever I condemn anyone—terrible (hmmm, same root as terrorist)—and the way I feel when I don't—peaceful, happy and free. I think most of us are busy either judging or loving, one or the other; it's pretty hard to do both at the same time.

And I'd forgotten all about that 7th grade party, but it was definitely one of the most painful nights of my young life. I thought it would never end; and I guess, in a way, as God suggested, it never did.

He's right about something else, too (or maybe about everything else; he *is* God, after all). I have let the opinions of others, no matter how cruel or untrue, color and even define me. How silly is that! I've given away my power, my love of myself and ultimately my love of others.

And I'm not alone; I'd bet most people or, at least, most girls and women—probably quite a few men, too—have. So, yes, I guess we become terrorists when we do that because we become afraid. And when you're afraid, you do things and say things and even think things that you wouldn't do or say or think otherwise. It's a choice we make without even realizing we're making it whenever we let fear take over our lives.

If only I could remember that when I go out into the world or when I'm sitting at home alone, brooding about things— because I don't want to be a terrorist anymore, not for a minute. I want to be happy, not terrified, in love with everyone in this whole, huge, beautiful world.

Thirteen

"Love, which created me, is what I am."
-A Course in Miracles

Okay, I understand. We're all terrorists, in a way. Once we start treating each other and ourselves better, we'll naturally create a more loving and peaceful world, right?

> Right. It may take time, but the good news is that positive energy actually neutralizes negative energy. Start with yourself, and let the rippling effect begin.

Okay, I'll try.

But here's another question for you about... (Get ready... two of your favorite words, I know)...about a different kind of 'separation' and 'loss': Why is it that some of us in this world lead comfortable lives financially and materially, whereas others have almost nothing? In the U.S., many of us—though not all, of course, especially during times of recession—can count on three meals a day, a decent shelter and the essentials of life, whereas so many others are not so fortunate. The biggest fear most Americans supposedly face is public speaking. How ironic is that compared to those in the world who fear starvation, torture or even death!

Help us to understand this inequity, God, especially since so many people are born into and live their whole lives in abject poverty and desolation. It seems so unfair.

> It's true that those of you who have so much financially and materially are blessed; and I know many of you are grateful and even desirous of sharing your abundance with those less fortunate. If you're one of those, look for ways and opportunities to do just that. Ask always, "How may I serve? How may I give back to my fellow man and to all beings in gratitude and in love?" And then seek to do that in word and deed with money, resources, smiles, tenderness and love. Heal all whose path you cross. Bless all, and share all you have. As you give, so shall you receive. As you love, so shall you be loved. As you heal, so shall you be healed.

I'm trying to do that. Lately I've made a commitment to give at least 10% of my income to those less fortunate, sometimes to individuals I know and sometimes to nonprofit or charitable groups no matter how tight my finances are. Usually if my checkbook balance is low, it's because I've spent too much on myself or my family anyway; so I figure if I have the money to spend on the 'extras' in life, I certainly have the money to give to others who have so much less than I have. I give one-third for people, one-third for animals and one-third for the environment.

I feel good about it, and somehow I always seem to have enough for groceries and bills—and so many other things.

> Yes, this is the surest test of happiness—how you feel, really feel, about what you do. Your giving makes you feel good and bolsters your state of joy. The satisfaction you gain, as much as the money and the time you give, adds to the happiness and well-being of the world.

I volunteer a little, too; but right now I'm spending lots of extra time both inside and outside of my classroom helping students with their papers, writing letters of recommendation and just being there for them when they need to talk. I expend tons of energy for them every day, especially on my 'Motivational Magic' days. They seem to look forward to those days and tell me they like the fact that I don't just teach them English but that I also teach them about life. Sometimes I use my life coaching skills, as well, with teenagers and adults and in community education classes. For now, those are the ways I volunteer.

Still, I know I could do more. I have so much...

> Be happy with what you do, Pam, and continue to open your heart to all the abundance that comes into your life, financially, emotionally, spiritually, intellectually, socially and in every other way. Never feel you don't deserve it or that in some way your share prevents others from having what they need. There's enough for all on this planet if only each of you would open yourselves to what IS, while finding ways to share it with others. When you see abundance flowing into your life, embrace it and give thanks. Be

responsible, but don't limit yourself unnecessarily for as you do, you exhibit fear. Never say, "I have too much," or, "Something bad must be coming with all this good." Never! Always expect good things to come, and surely goodness and mercy shall follow you all the days of your life.

You know, it's funny you say that, God, but sometimes I find that I'm as stressed if my bank account balance is high as I am when it's low. I wonder at those times if somehow I've ended up with more than I deserve. It's the way I've always felt up until now, that I should have enough to pay my bills and maybe a little extra for savings, but not so much that I can be extravagant. My fear of success is as great as my fear of failure, I think. Maybe I still feel unworthy.

Feel that way no longer, Pam. Expect much, allow much, realizing that with the acceptance of abundance comes the ability to give more.

With each gift—a raise in salary, a sunset, a song—give thanks. As you do, you'll receive more and more, and you'll find ways to share more and more with others. Never hoard your possessions, your smiles, your affection or your love. Make the world a better place for your having lived. Remember that you chose this life—your status, your family, your position. You can continue to choose throughout this lifetime and forever after. Choose abundance, if you will. Choose love, never fear or lack or limitation—unless, of course, that's what you want. The choice is always yours.

As I've said before, others have selected their lot

in life before ever coming to this earth. Even the role of poverty that some have embraced will serve their healing. Trust that, and be at peace. However, your desire to end scarcity and to share your resources becomes a means of healing, too, for others but even more so for you. Give, give and give if that's what feels right to you. Accept all abundance graciously and lovingly, and give back graciously and lovingly to all.

The world is waiting. This is the life you've chosen, and that is the life of another. Each has its blessings and each, its crosses, opportunities all. You, Pam, are Spirit; and so is your brother, whether his belly be empty or full. You've come to save the world, and so have your sisters and brothers, each in their own way. The universe, which is I, will show each of you how.

Remember, too, that abundance comes in many guises, in smiles, in laughter, in a kind word, in a kiss. Allow your abundance, all of it, to flow out into the world. Trust yourself and trust me. With God, you know, all things are possible. With Pam, all things are possible, too; and so it is with all your brothers and sisters. Only open your hearts, your eyes and your souls to the goodness in the world; stretch out your hands and bless all you touch.

Ask yourself this question: Do I want this goodness? Your answer will determine whether you live a life of abundance or a life of scarcity. It is a simple law of physics: What you focus on is what you get. If you want abundance, think abundant thoughts. Concentrate on that which is good in your life, and it will expand. Higher, faster-moving energy—that

which comprises abundance and love, for example—
naturally dissolves slower-moving energy of scarcity
and fear. When you're happy, you're strong; when
you're sad, you're weak. It's all about the flow of
energy.

Look for the blessings in your life; they're
everywhere. Be appreciative always.   Awareness,
Appreciation and Awe, the three A's, are such
important keys to happiness and success.

I love you. I love all my children, my creations,
no matter what you choose—abundance or scarcity,
joy or fear. Know this. I love you... always.

Fourteen

"All things are lessons God would have me learn."
-A Course in Miracles

Today was a mess, God. I was grumpy all day with my students, and lately I've felt irritable and depressed. I don't want to be this way anymore. I want to be kind always, not just when I happen to be in a good mood. Whenever I'm reading inspirational books or meditating, everything seems so obvious, so simple; but when I'm out in the world, dealing with people, paperwork, messy situations, I so often forget who I really am and who I want to be. I say and do what seems most expedient or efficient at the time but what is, in retrospect, not the best or most compassionate way of dealing with the situation. I become overwhelmed and far from present. Help me to more completely evolve into the person you created. Help me to be my authentic self.

Again, I say to you, Pam, and to all my children,
if you want to be truly happy, practice the vow of

Ahimsa. Do nothing to harm anyone through word or action—anyone, and that means your students, your colleagues, your family, your friends AND yourself. Lately you've allowed yourself to withdraw from others a bit; you've become detached and introspective. Never allow this, even for a moment, since you obviously regret it afterwards.

Practice. But notice what you're practicing, and be sure it's what you want. Are you practicing the art of criticizing or complaining? Are you practicing feeling overwhelmed or sorry for yourself? Or are you practicing the skills of clarity, compassion and kindness for others and yourself? 'Practice makes perfect,' they say. So you may wish to reevaluate what it is you're practicing.

Have courage. It takes courage to be kind even when you feel testy, courage to smile and extend yourself to others even when you feel isolated or alone. Be courageous. Let no opportunity pass when you might have made a positive difference in the life of another. Each day look for ways to make the world a better place. Reach out to all. Take an interest in all. Look into your brothers' and sisters' eyes and see in them yourself and me. As you do, as you see, truly see, you'll find it impossible to be anything but kind.

And yet be gentle with yourself. Reflect on your day. Was there no one you helped? Surely you remember at least one. I saw you smile at nearly every one of your students at some time today. I saw you stop in the hallways and speak a kind word or two to many, and I heard you joke with several of your colleagues. Perhaps you don't remember; I wonder sometimes why you dwell on your faults so much when you have so many good and admirable qualities if only you'd notice them. You seem to see them in others. See them in yourself, as well.

But continue to do all you can to ensure that those brothers or sisters who come into your presence feel better about themselves when they depart. As you see in them their beauty and reflect it back to them, you'll help them rise above their troubles and construct a world that is a better place for all. Your kindness will ripple outward, creating circles of light that will encapsulate the earth. As the rustle of a butterfly's wings creates a breeze halfway across the planet, so, too, will any act of kindness and love. If only my children would realize this and instead of saying, "What can one person do?" say instead, "I will do whatever I can."

Be yourself, truly your authentic, eternal Self, and you'll rise above all earthly cares to that which exceeds your greatest hopes. You'll raise your energy levels to love, joy, peace and enlightenment. These are inside you at all times; you have only to access them. Your mind, like a computer, is packed full of information; but without a password, you cannot access it. Access it now with Love.

I want to, God. And right now, as I talk to you, it seems possible. But then when I go out into the world, I get so enmeshed in whatever's going on that I forget to be my best self. I react irritably at times, judge others and forget to see the real person in front of me. It's hard to change the behavior of a lifetime.

Let's face it. I'm not perfect, God, and never will be. I wish I were, wish I could be, but I can't. It's that simple, but it's frustrating, too.

You're perfect to me, Pam, to the God who made you; and so are all of your brothers and sisters, All of them, All beings, All Creation. PERFECT.

Look ahead to the end of your earthly life for a moment. What exactly do you want to have accomplished by then? What would you want others to think about you when you're no longer here—that you were kind, or that you were sometimes kind? That you made a difference in their lives, or that you were too moody or wrapped up in your own life to notice them? What do you hope others will say about you at your memorial service and ever afterward? Think about those things; perhaps even write them down. Then begin living your life in a way that will allow it to unfold as you would wish, and treat others in the way you want to be treated, with joy and kindness and love.

It's not hard.

So many people think they have no control over their thoughts and feelings, that their minds control them. They're mistaken. They have only to take charge—first, to become aware of their ideas and emotions and then to mold them into what they want. Accept the thoughts you have, or create new ones. Think of happy times, loved ones, beauty, anything positive. Watch your energy shift until you feel happy inside. If a negative thought occurs, counter it with a positive one or simply be with that thought, realizing it's just that—a thought not a fact, a transitory, fleeting mind-event that will pass. You don't belong to your mind; it belongs to you. Lead it gently and joyfully, as you would guide a child. Eventually, you and your mind will become one, inseparable, seeking the same thing, which is happiness.

Go inside and find Happiness there now. It's waiting for you. I'm waiting for you. I who am Love, Light, Laughter, Peace and Joy—I am with you always, no matter how you're feeling or behaving. I don't stop being with you just because you're angry or fearful or even cruel. You're an expression of the Divine. Remember that; and for God's sake— literally—love your Self and all Creation.

You're never apart from me or from anyone or anything else really, for all things are God-essence— the sky, the chair you're sitting on, the very cells that make up your body. I love you; I love All, All Creation, always.

Fifteen

"Speak to us, Father, that we may be healed."
-A Course in Miracles

Okay, I'm trying, God. But despite everything, life seems pretty dreary right now. I put on a good front when I'm with others—that's something, I guess—but inside I'm feeling pretty low. I wake up to blue skies and see gray. I read words on a page that blur. I keep thinking, what does any of this matter anymore? I sleep fitfully and little, and the dark circles under my eyes grow darker.

Why can't I heal, Father? It's been almost a year since John and I split up. I know my problems are insignificant compared to many others. And I have SO MUCH! I know that, all of that! So WHY can't I get on with my life and be happy?

I keep thinking: Like so much rubbish, I've been cast away by the man I loved, as have so many other women before me. What is it with men when they reach the age of 40 or 50? Is it a species survival thing? It makes sense that once upon a time men needed to experience their 'mid-life crisis' and procreate with younger women so the human species could flourish, but that time is long past. Our species is crowding out the rest of the world, so why do men continue to behave in this way? Why don't they evolve responsibly? Or just grow up!

Okay, okay, I know I'm sounding bitter now. And I am!

Lately I accomplish little and have a hard time focusing, even on my discussions with you. Is everything a sham? Are you a sham? Well, not you, God, but your talking to me? Am I just fooling myself so I can survive this pain?

I'm not sure of anything anymore, other than I feel sad and worthless and utterly alone right now. Please help me, God. Help me to understand.

As I've said before and will say again as many times as it takes, you're never alone, Pam. If you knew who walked beside you, sat beside you, hovered around you and all others even now, you'd know that all is well, that you're fine, that you can have, be and do anything you wish at any time.

As you've admitted, you have so much. Perhaps you should stop looking at what you think is missing and see what's here, right now. You sit in a cozy home, gazing out the window at such beauty—blue sky speckled with the pink clouds of sunrise, snow on pine and spruce, two little dogs that are utterly devoted to you nosing their way about the yard, your two sons, safe and asleep in their warm beds.

Yes, your husband has left. Yes, your life is in transition. Yes, some of the illusory securities have crumbled away. But they were, after all, only illusions. Dust to dust, ashes to ashes, illusion to illusion. Illusions evaporate, you know. They vanish, as do all mirages. They were never real to begin with, so why would they not?

You, however, live on. Sometimes events in life don't exactly seem fortuitous, yet each is perfect. You created them in your perfection, the perfection which, by the way, encompasses your frailties and heartaches, as well as your strengths and joys. The moments you've danced with another in complete bliss or laughed until your sides have ached are no more beautiful than the moments you've cried in anguish or cringed inside at the recognition of your errors. Each is glorious in its own way, for each brings a kind of blessing.

Remember, for example, your last birthday when you drove to the mountains and camped with only your two dogs at your side. You sat under a star-flecked sky, listening to the silence and feeling a joy unspeakable, despite your pain, as you melted into timelessness and became one with the Source of all. With Me. Years ago, when you were a young woman struggling with a full-time job, a family and depression, in a moment of conflict, you said to your sons these words that you never imagined you would say to them or to anyone: "I hate your guts!" (Yes, I see that you're blushing in embarrassment, even now.) The words sprang from your lips before you could stop them; and you paused, horrified that you could even think such thoughts, let alone express them to those you loved. Though you apologized repeatedly, you carried forever afterward the look of startled amazement that you saw in their eyes. Years later, when your youngest son Will reminded you laughingly of this event, you dissolved into tears at the knowledge that he still remembered it and cried out to your family for forgiveness. How blessed that moment was when at last you were able to let down your defenses and give and receive healing. Both the night of ecstasy under the stars and the night of tears at home were equally perfect for your soul.

All is well, my child, though you may not perceive it now. Yet know it. As your life and heart evolve, so does your ability to rise above seeming adversities. You'll soon laugh at them, knowing they're the greatest illusions of all. They will crumble. You, however, will not, for you are eternal.

I am here. This is I. Believe it. You seem to feel that it should take great effort to commune with God. It takes no effort, at all, for I am within you, beside you, above and around you. I am you, and you are an intrinsic and very important part of me forever. You are the white clouds that drift overhead. You are the blue sky. I am the snow on the spruce and the wind in your hair.

Arise. Laugh. Love. Open your heart, Pam. Awaken to the promise of winter for under the snow lies grass, asleep perhaps but very much alive, and the golden brown bulbs of springtime that will poke their heads up through the dark earth and burst forth exactly at the right instant. You've heard the saying, "Faith is the note the songbird makes before the dawn." Be the songbird now; in faith, sing.

Arise, my dear and all my beloved children. Awaken. Appreciate all. Life is yours forever. So even now, before dawn, sing.

Another sleepless night...

I throw back the covers, traipse down the stairs and crack open the front door. Cold air rushes in, but it feels good. Barefoot and all, I slip into the darkness and disappear with the night.

Silence envelops me. It's good to be out here under the sky, alone except for the few creatures that have decided to stick around for the winter. I hear a rustling overhead, just the tiny sound of some feathered thing settling more comfortably on its perch, and far above me comes the whistle of wings as a flock of geese glide eerily by.

Nature is the Great Mother who cradles us in her arms. She has been my salvation through this ordeal. Whether I sleep tonight or not, I will get up in the morning as I always do and race along frozen mountain trails. As long as I keep moving, I'm fine.

For now, this is perfect, this invisible dwelling, this just-being in the wondrous, mystical magic of night.

Sixteen

"God, grant me the serenity to accept the things I cannot change, the courage to change the things I can, and the wisdom to know the difference."
-AA Prayer

God, I need your help again. I'm sorry, but the world seems so dark to me today. Last night I felt some hope, but now I don't want to go on...

And yet you must, not because I say so but because you do, because you will it deep within the core of your being. Go past the darkness, Pam, and choose light. Don't react—act! Be your most loving self, your highest self, right here and right now. As you do, joy will inevitably well up within you.

You have begun a journey of enlightenment and peace, a journey of love, a journey of joy. Sometimes it takes a few jump starts to get an engine going; but once started, it will coast, slowly at first, and then it will roll and sputter and finally catch. So it is with those of you who grieve. If you but believe, despite the darkness, if you persist and have faith, you'll ride through the fog past the circle of fire to the source of all passion and light, to that which is divine, that which is within and around you, that which is a part of you, of all creation and of me. And then joy unspeakable will be yours.

But, Father, it doesn't last. One minute I'm hopeful; and then the next, I'm right back where I was before—in the depths of hell. I never thought my life would be like this. I never thought John would abandon me. I just never thought...

Be at peace, Pam, and in all things, follow your heart. Whether you know it or not, others sense a new you, independent and energized, and are attracted. Even John is, in his own way. He pretends, even to himself, that he's not; but he is.

I wish I could believe that. With all my heart, I do.

Be patient, my lamb. All is well. You've asked for healing for both of you and for the world. Healing is occurring, though in truth no healing is necessary for that which is eternal, that which is you—and John and all others—that which is God. Though it may not be clear to you now, nevertheless know that the mist is rising and will continue to dissolve before your very eyes. Your vision is clearing as you realize that above all else, above even a reconciliation of your marriage, you want to see things as they are; you want Truth.

Yes, I do want that. I want it even more than I want John.

I'm glad, for with truth comes light. In the greater scheme of things, it's not really important what happens between you and John or between you and anyone else, for that matter. What is important is that you love all. Simply love them, each and every one. Concern yourself only with matters over which you have control, matters of the heart, *YOUR* heart.

This dark time is an opportunity if you will but take it. Believe. Hope. Love. Laugh. Trust. And let the joy ride begin!

Seventeen

"If any man be in Christ, he is a new creature: old things are passed away; behold all things are become new."
-II Corinthians 5:17

Another day. And I'm so sad again, Father. I feel like I'm on an emotional roller coaster, one moment up and the next down—way down. I haven't been sleeping much, so it all becomes a vicious cycle. No sleep, depression; depression, no sleep.

The bottom line is this: I want my life back—only not the way it was. I want a new life, with awareness and gratitude. I want no less than a miracle, and I want it today. I know I'm asking a lot, God, but I'm asking it anyway. Heal my heart, John's heart, our marriage. Help us to love again.

Or, at the very least, help me to let John go. Completely. Forever. At last.

Will you, God? Will you help me?

...I can't hear you.

Please, please answer me...

I'm here, always here in your heart, Pam, in the hearts of all my children. What can I say to help you understand? You want John to come back—today; and if he doesn't, you want complete freedom, for him and from him. Is that it?

Yes.

Freedom forever.

Yes.

It's not possible, you know, what you've requested. Oh, it's possible that John will awaken this morning and discover that he's been asleep this last year. That he's inextricably connected to you, always has been and always will be. And he is. And so are the trees outside, and the wind, and the rivers rushing through canyons and cascading down snow-covered cliffs to the valleys below. And so am I. Yes, we are all inextricably and forever entwined.

But, of course, you're speaking of something beyond even this. And you're asking for a miracle. And so I say to you, yes. Believe it. John does love you. He will always love you, though he may deny it in his heart for all time. For the last eighteen years, he has denied it, in a way. Perhaps even before that, for even early on he resisted marriage and all of its obligations. He has felt trapped. He has wished to spread his wings and fly.

Do you see this? Do you see how his soul has felt bound to earth in his relationship with you? It was why he came home so late at night so many times and why he spent so little time with you over the last several years.

It was a kind of immaturity, a fear of death and mortality, a need to fly unfettered.

He thinks his freedom from the marriage allows this flight. But it does not. It is helping to heal his wings, give him strength. But the sky he flies in at present is a bit empty of stardust and substance.

When he is ready, he will come back, perhaps as your husband, perhaps as a dear friend, perhaps in another way altogether. But he will come back. I cannot say it will be today, though I do not say it will not be, for miracles happen—but only when they happen in your heart; in John's, too, but especially, in this case, in yours. When you can indeed laugh despite all seeming loss and unhappiness—all illusion—that will be the day John will return. And all the heavens will sing. John will be free in a way he never imagined when he comes back to you, perhaps because he will have come back to me, too, and to the world and, especially—yes, especially—to himself. You will fly, too. You will have realized by then that it is your own happiness that lifts you up into the sky, your own song that carries you to heaven. How beautiful to share your life with a loved one, but how much more glorious to love yourself as much. Begin today the greatest love affair of your life, Pam, the love affair with YOU, with the authentic, beautiful You.

Today. Yes, today. For eternity begins today. Be patient no more. Let the miracle instant begin! But let it begin with YOU.

Eighteen

"This is the refreshing."
-Isaiah 28:12

As I was cross-country skiing today, God, I looked around and caught a glimpse of what you've been telling me. The plants, amazingly still green and alive in the icy stream, were slender and graceful below me; the water, crystal clear yet hazy blue with ice; the snow-covered fields, the mountains and sky; my two cute dogs trailing behind me; the whole world lovely and majestic; and all of us one, beautiful because we reflect each other and mirror You—You, who have so perfectly created us.

Yes, we, you, all are one. Remember that, and you'll never feel lonely or alone. The skiers out beyond that bend are one with you, too. They're happy and alive, and so are you as you share, consciously and unconsciously, their joy. You're beginning to feel that, aren't you? Even when you're far away in terms of miles, your soul communes with all. As your brother dances, you dance. As your sister cries, you cry. You are all one.

And think of this: You're all a part of me, such an important part that I'd be incomplete without you. I who am All-Love, All-Power, All-Everything love you so much that I—God—would be less than perfect without you. Some who will read this may think you're being irreverent and arrogant to write such words—God incomplete, less than perfect without you or me or anyone? Impossible!

And yet, I tell you it is true. Think about it. Are you complete without your loved ones or even your acquaintances? The answer to that is twofold. On the one hand, you are indeed complete, whole and perfect, in and of yourself. You always will be. On the other hand, all the shared moments of tenderness, compassion and even anger bind you forever. If you, then, are incomplete without those who have crossed your path and touched your soul, so, too, am I who encompass and embody Perfect Love.

It's not arrogance, at all, but rather perfection. How could I, God, not love my Creations so completely as to want you to complete me? Yet, in the Divine Paradox, I Am always complete, always perfect. And so are you. Now, that is unconditional, nonjudgmental, perfect Love. That, in fact, is God!

---DANIEL 5/7:Daniel

Change   10.00
                0.00

Have a nice day!

Od1

111991540003

Nineteen

"One must not cease from exploration; and the end of all our exploring will be to arrive where we began and to know the place for the first time."
-T. S. Eliot

Dear Friend (I hope that doesn't seem irreverent, but I feel I can call you that; tell me if I shouldn't),

Today I released John from my heart, at least for now. Every time I thought of him, I sent love to him with my best wishes; and then I let him go.

"Goodbye, John," I said, and meant it. "I love you. I love you so much that I'm setting you free. I bless you and all who cross your path, and I hope you find whatever—and whomever—you're seeking. As I let go of our relationship, I free myself and move on at last."

Thanks for helping me to arrive at this place, God.

You're welcome, my dear one, my friend indeed.
And yes, you're correct. As you set John free, you

free yourself. No one can be happy who feels tied to earth. Only through flight, through freedom and through the eternal loosening of all bonds can we soar. When you try to bind someone else, remember that you must hold one end of the cord, and that binds you, as well. Let go, and you both will feel the wind in your hair and the sky beneath your wings. Freedom is indeed bliss. All the angels will soar with you.

As I've said before, I... we—the angels and all the hosts of heaven—choose your highest good; but even more, we choose your will, for that's the surest measure of love. That's why it's good you've chosen John's will, why you've sent and blessed him on his way.

Though you may feel John betrayed you and his marriage vows, you must realize that nothing is ever so simple as that. True, he promised to love and be true to you forever. His choice to leave seems not to honor this commitment. And yet, I say to you, do not judge him, for above all he must be true to his soul. If his Authentic Self is crying out to him to explore a new path, he must do so. To do otherwise would be a grave error indeed, for he has come to earth, as you and all of your brothers and sisters have, to heal and, especially, to remember who he truly is, to deepen—to reawaken—his ability to love fully. Even as he breaks faith with the promise he made to you years ago, he must forgive and love himself, despite what you or anyone else might think. Only as he loves himself can he love you and others deeply.

I know; I've tried to forgive him.

You must forgive him—*truly* forgive, not for his sake but for your own. You must see past his apparent failings to that which is Eternal, Perfect, Beautiful and True, to that which is God Myself within John. Only as you forgive will you be free to love and trust again.

Never judge another, Pam. How can you possibly know what's in the heart of your brother when you seem not to know, at times, what's inside your own? You've both been the betrayer and the betrayed. Over the years, your erratic thoughts, feelings and moods have shifted much like the sands along a windy shoreline. Forgive yourself for that, and forgive John, as well. Each of you has done what your soul has cried out to you to do. Perhaps the pain you've experienced this past year will help you both gain wisdom and depth. For now, know only that John is not able to find himself in his marriage to you—anymore, as a matter of fact, than you're able to find yourself there.

However, I caution you and all who read this. One must never take what I say here lightly, just as one must never take one's commitment to another lightly. These words do not serve as a license to betray another at the slightest whim. No, never, for to do so would be a betrayal, not only of another, but of one's deepest self.

This situation between you and John is not a case of an instant's betrayal. This is a case of trying and failing and trying again over many years. This is a case of each of you wanting to love the other, yearning to show that love, yet finding it impossible to do so, for whatever reasons. This is a case of prolonged frustration and discontent. Together you could not find the way; apart, you're learning to do so. Perhaps the time will come when you'll reclaim love's pulse and passion with each other; perhaps not. The important thing is that, together or apart, you will each discover it.

John is on a journey, and he has propelled you on one, as well. Give him thanks, for you'll travel to places beyond any you have yet known. It is a journey of the heart, a path to your truest selves, a road leading home.

Praise Heaven—and John—that the two of you have begun this sojourn, at last.

Reflections…

I've been experimenting over the last few weeks with the idea of seeing my thoughts just as thoughts and not as the absolute facts I always assumed they were. And, boy oh boy, has that been interesting!

It's as though my thoughts grab hold of me by the hand, like they're my best friends and all; and then the next thing I know, they've led me to some of the darkest, most depressing corners of the world—and they're all in my mind. One minute I'll be thinking about my sons and how wonderful they are, then the next I'll be blaming myself because they no longer have the stable family they once had, and the next I'll be filled with self-loathing because I let my marriage fall apart, and the next I'll be back in the past at one of my son's basketball games, correcting papers instead of really watching the game every second the way a good mother would and blaming myself for that, and the next… Well, it goes on and on. My mind has become a monster that doesn't seem to belong to me anymore, and I have become its slave.

But lately, ever since God mentioned in a discussion we had a few weeks ago that our minds don't control us unless we let them, I've been noticing my thoughts without trying to fix them, simply observing them and seeing what they are and where they're taking me. I don't always remember to do this; but when I do, I just stop for a minute and go inside to see what's happening there—what I'm thinking, how I'm feeling, how my body's reacting to it all. Mostly, when I'm thinking negative thoughts, I feel a kind of burning and churning in or around my solar plexus. But when I actually take a moment to pause and notice, some of the uneasiness dissipates. Interesting!

I've also begun to realize that so many of my thoughts are just part of a tape I've been playing over and over in my mind for as long as I can remember, a tape that's not necessarily accurate. For example, I really was a good mother and still am. Yes, I'm a busy working mother, an English teacher who has lots of papers to correct, but a supportive and loving mother, too, who's always there at all my sons' games and performances, watching with rapt attention far more than correcting papers. Anyway, I've started talking back to that tape in my mind. "Oh, it's you again," I say, "my critic who thinks I'm the cause of everything that's gone wrong in the world." Or, "Oh, here's my 'you're-just-not-good-enough' tape again. You know, I'm getting a little tired of your music. Maybe I'll put on a different tune."

Unfortunately, I don't always catch myself until after I've fallen into this huge crevasse of worthlessness and depression. But even then if I stop to observe what's happening inside, I find I'm usually not quite so stuck in the mire as I was before. My 'best friends' are still there trying to drag me down, but at least I'm not as inclined to believe everything they tell me about myself or my life or about life, in general. Just this new little bit of questioning and observing has helped me see things—myself and others and my relationships—more compassionately.

And compassion... well, whenever I view this life of mine—and those of others—from a place of compassion, I find the scenery quite extraordinary, after all!

Twenty

"When ye stand praying, forgive, if ye have aught against any."
–Mark 11:25

Several weeks have passed since we last spoke, God. I've neglected you, pushing our discussions further and further back on my daily schedule until I'm too exhausted to talk. I've saved you until last instead of making you a priority first thing in the morning. Forgive me; I'll try to do better from now on.

It's good to hear from you again, Pam, though in truth you've been with me—and I with you—all along. Yes, you do fill the hours with busy things. You DO so much every day. Why is that? You make long lists then cross each item off, one by one; and only then do you feel you've lived your life well. Perhaps if you DID less, at times, and focused on BEING more, you'd find the peace and happiness that so often eludes you. Consider that.

As for my forgiveness, dear friend, you have it,

though I can truly say that there's nothing to forgive. Nor, quite honestly, do I even know how to forgive since I see *nothing* that requires 'forgiveness'— empathy, yes, and compassion, caring, kindness. Try to understand that I see only you, the real you and all of my children just as you are, as you've always been and as you always shall be, as I created you. "You are one Self, united with your creator and all aspects of creation, unlimited in power and in peace." *-A Course in Miracles* You are your One Self, which is the compilation of Me and all Humankind and all Creation, which is perfect and beautiful and true.

Forgiveness is important for you and your brothers and sisters in this earthly life; however, it's inconsequential—nonexistent, in fact—for me, for I see past appearance to the reality that is you, the reality that is Love. Your putting me off does not offend me, for I cannot be offended. I can only love you, and I do. Try to remember as you go about the business—the busy-ness—of the day to bring me into that business, into that moment—this moment, which is all there is, now and forever. Thus, you will BE more than you will DO; and all that you DO will be gifted by Love, Compassion and Peace. As you see the light that automatically comes with this, you'll accomplish and BE so much. With light comes strength; with strength, defenselessness; with defenselessness, peace; with peace, joy; with joy, love. And so the circle continues.

Be love. Be you. Be the light in which others see their beauty, their perfect holiness, the joy of their perfect Selves. Yes, for as you do, you will find that elusive quality called happiness. You will know your Self then, and you will Be as you have always Been— You, the changeless You, the eternal You, the You that is also Me, and John, and your children, and the moth that lights upon both flower and weed, and the rain that falls upon thistle and rose, all one, all creation.

Welcome back, though in truth you've never been away. All is well. All is well. All is indeed and forevermore well!

Twenty-One

"... Choose instead a gentle listening to the word of God. He speaks from nearer than your heart to you. His voice is closer than your hand. Love is everything you are and that He is; the same as you and you the same as He."
-A Course in Miracles

Good morning, God. Thank you for a good night's rest. How wonderful that simple blessing is! Thanks for chats with friends and for the moonlit cross-country ski with my dogs last night, for the sifting fog and haunting echoes on one side and the starlit slit of sky on the other. This world you've created is so beautiful.

Why is it that the sky brings me so close to you with all its cloud messages sent directly from Heaven? I look up and see such beauty there and everywhere in nature—the sunset, the stars, the mountains, the frost upon the trees. They sing to my soul.

Nature is the great healer. It's my hand reaching out to bless and touch you all. Go outside often and feel its balm upon your soul. Watch out for your world, your mother who has suckled and cared so tenderly for all of you, all humanity and all other beings, as well. Oh, if you could only see how gently she walks beside you, you'd know you have nothing to fear.

Yes, I feel that when I'm outside. It's almost as if the trees, the birds, even the rocks—all aspects of Nature—send out peace and love to me if only I open my heart and listen.

Your planet, the ground beneath your feet, the air you breathe—all are as holy as the souls who minister as angels to each of you. Show reverence to all, all humanity and all of nature. Care for Mother Earth as you would your own earthly mother if she'd been injured. For this mother has certainly been wounded over and over again. She's worn and abused and terribly misunderstood. She needs you now more than ever.

Yes, and I realize my species, the "most intelligent species," is responsible for so much of this abuse—and I'm as guilty as anyone. We 'Baby Boomers' grew up thinking our resources would last forever. We're beginning to learn otherwise, and many of us are trying to do things differently. We've got a long way to go, though.

I'm glad you recognize this; and I hope you'll see all creation as a part of Mother Earth and treat all animals and plants and insects, all species, all organisms with reverence and respect. In so doing, you offer yourself that same blessing. The *Bible* talks about man having dominion over all. But with true dominion comes a duty, not to use and abuse other species on your planet but to treat all with compassion and with kindness.

Many think I love the human species more than any other, but I tell you I love all equally, all creation. Every dog, every cat, every person, every sparrow, every flower, every rock, every blade of grass—each is as dear to me as another. I am God. I am Love. How then could I possibly favor one creation over another? I cannot. I do not. All are part of the great fabric of Life, a tapestry with multi-colored threads. You and I and All Beings are one.

Even snakes and spiders?

Even snakes and spiders.

I'm kidding. I used to be afraid of them, but now... well, I guess I'm a little afraid, but not like I once was. What happened was this: One night when I was a little girl, I heard the chirping of a cricket behind my dresser. I screamed until my older brother came to my rescue.

"The poor little cricket," he said, pulling the dresser out from the wall. "Here it is, minding its own business, not hurting anyone; and you want me to kill it. I'll bet it has babies outside just waiting for their mother to come home and take care of them. But now they'll never see her again because of you."

I stopped crying and stood still, terrified at the idea of sharing my bedroom with a cricket but troubled by the horrific thing I was asking him to do.

"Don't kill it," I relented. "Just capture it and take it outside."

But he was enjoying my suffering. "Oh, no," he said. "You told me to kill it. And since I'm such a good brother, I will."

"No," I begged him. "Don't kill it. Please don't kill it."

Desperate, I even suggested he leave it right where it was. I could sleep with it in the room if I had to, I insisted.

But he wouldn't listen. Extracting the terrified creature from its hiding place, he placed it within full view of me and squashed it. I was horrified and feel guilty to this day for my part in that senseless killing.

The lesson has stayed with me. Today I fear regret more than I fear most any living creature, or anything else, for that matter, and try hard to be kind to all. My children, too, have learned this lesson. We keep a jar and a piece of cardboard handy so that we can carefully transport to the great outdoors any multi-legged insect friends who are tempted to move in with us. Though we don't necessarily encourage their occupancy, we wish our fellow creatures only the best, certainly no harm, and try to do what we can to keep them safe.

Yes, be kind, Pam, but never out of fear of anything—snakes, spiders, crickets, pollution, dwindling resources, even regrets. Fear is the absence of love. As you bring love to your heart, you bring it to all others and to the world, as well. What can you do to help Mother Earth, you ask, and I answer, "Love. Just love. Always. Let that be your guide."

Only love will save your world now, your species and all of Life. Only love can bring a Heaven to Earth.

Twenty-Two

"When you become quiet, it just dawns on you."
–Thomas Edison

Here's another question for you, God, one I think many of us ask ourselves from time to time: What's my mission on earth? How can I best serve you and others while I'm here? And how do we ever really know whether or not we've accomplished it?

Your mission is whatever you decide it will be, Pam, and it has already begun. You're asking questions and listening to the answers that come from your heart. You're finding your own way. That's enough for now.

Your path is the one you tread; your life, the one you create. It's your...

I know—it's my choice, right?

Yes, your choice. Always.

Twenty-Three

"I can elect to change all thoughts that hurt."
-A Course in Miracles

I'm a little depressed today, God. I started out feeling hopeful, but now I'm full of doubts and fears again, and for no good reason. I do miss my husband.

It's not as though I don't have enough to do or people in my life to do them with. I had two dates yesterday, if you want to call them that, and plenty of other things on my agenda. But still I feel sad. What's wrong with me? Why can't I get on with my life? Why do I hold on so tightly to what used to be?

You can get on with life if you choose to, Pam. It's that simple. Choose. Instead of focusing on what's wrong in your life, notice what's right. Then your illusions—and that's all your misperceptions are, illusions—will diminish. Remember, as I've said before, a perceived trouble is but a mist, a cloud that momentarily veils the sun. The sun is always there. It's only hidden for a while behind the mist. When you refuse to let your troubles cover what you know is true, you'll see the Truth, the sun, always shining, always there.

I know. But when it feels this dark...

This is not your first dark time, Pam, nor will it be your last—unless, of course, you make that choice. Don't you remember, for example, when you were 17, a senior in high school, living with your sister in an apartment? You'd left your home and friends behind to move to another city so you could establish residency before college. You were lonely then, too.

Yes, that was one of the hardest times of my life.

Let's go back to it then. Perhaps you'll see that even in the darkest times, one can discern the light.

Maybe...
But it was so long ago that it feels almost as if that girl were someone else. It's easier to remember it that way...

Yes, but do remember it. It will help.

All right. I'll try...

...I see the girl in that new place, the 'me' that used to be. I see how difficult it was for her that year, making a new life for herself and getting used to the fact that she wouldn't exactly be the center of attention her last year of high school. Actually, she tried hard at first; she ran for an office, joined a club or two and made new friends. Her cousin, who lived nearby, became her best and closest friend, next to her sister; and the girl told her everything—about her past, her heartaches, her fears, her dreams for the future. She met a boy who took her to dances and kissed her and told her he loved her. In her loneliness, she thought maybe she loved him, too.

Months passed; and then one day, she found out a terrible thing. The two people she'd given her heart to in this new home, her cousin and her boyfriend, were seeing each other behind her back. They'd betrayed her, a betrayal that had been going on for a long time, she discovered. She could hardly believe it. She was alone now, more alone than she'd ever been in her life, especially since she had no mother or father to turn to, to comfort her, to tell her this dark time would pass. She began to believe it would never pass.

One day, she stood in front of the medicine cabinet and thought about the pills inside that could bring her the peace she longed for, that could take her away from this dark and empty place where she felt no love. But she didn't take them, not that day and not the next. I'm not sure why she didn't; but for then, at least, she didn't. She just kept moving forward as best she could and breathing and hoping from one moment to the next and the next. Her parents and siblings would have wanted her to, she knew, and so she did.

Each morning, she forced herself up despite the emptiness, forced herself to dress and eat breakfast and walk out the door for school, taking one step and then another and another, first one day and then the next and the next. Sometimes she'd see her old boyfriend in the hallways at school, and a wave of depression would crash over her. He'd smile at her, and she'd look away and wonder how she'd ever be able to go on. But she did go on, minute by minute, hour by hour, day by day.

One morning, several months later, she opened her eyes, looked out her window and saw the sun peeking over the mountaintop, painting the sky purple and gold. The next day, she noticed how crisp and clean the air was and saw the sunshine sparkling on the snow. She could breathe again, and smile. She was even able to laugh. And the world didn't seem so dark any more.

Yes, Pam, and laugh she did many times after that. She finished high school and went on to college, where she spent four of the happiest years of her life. She climbed mountain peaks, kissed boys, skied powdery slopes, hiked by moonlight, dreamed dreams, fell in love, married, had children, traveled around the world and lived fully and well.

And yet, she might have missed it all, missed so much, all because of one dark time, a fleeting instant, a speck in eternity that passed, as this dark time will, too.

Very soon now, when she wakes up in the morning, she'll get excited about all the adventures that lay ahead. Having moved so far into the darkness, she'll savor the light. When she skis, she'll notice the cold rush of wind against her hair. When she hikes, she'll drink in the beauty of mountain lakes all around. When she lingers by the fire, she'll see her dogs sleeping beside her, and her sons, her family, her friends. She'll listen to the music and watch the flames and look about at her home and feel so lucky to be alive. She'll live in the present and look to the future with confidence and hope and give thanks for the memories and lessons of the past.

You are that girl from long ago. You have been acquainted with the night, but more often you have awakened to the sweet scent of morning and the dawning of light.

Awaken now, Pam. Believe. Sing. Give thanks. For you and all my children are indeed so very blessed.

Twenty-Four

"What we once enjoyed and deeply loved we can never lose, for all that we love deeply becomes part of us."
–Helen Keller

I received a call this morning, God, a call of anguish. The husband of a dear friend died last night of a massive heart attack. She's beside herself with grief and can't imagine going on without her beloved Martin.

This was Kristen's second marriage, and it was long and good. She believes she can never love anyone the way she loved Martin. She's inconsolable.

What would you say to her at this dark time, God? What comfort can you give to her and to all who have lost a partner or spouse to death?

I would say to Kristen and to all, "I love you."

I would say that though she doesn't think she can go on, she will go on. And though she doesn't know it now, she will love another, maybe not in the exact same way as she loved Martin. But, I ask you, Pam, must anything be exactly the same? No snowflake, no fingerprint, no relationship, no anything is ever quite the same; all are unique, and all are equally filled with possibility and promise. She will love again in exactly the right way at exactly the right time. And she will be happy...

...if she chooses to be, of course. Only then. For the choice is always hers—and yours—never mine.

I would also say to Kristen and to all that there is no death, only life forevermore. Martin has not left her. How could he, loving her as much as he did on this earth? No, it is not possible.

I would say to this lovely woman of light and love, "Not only will you indeed find another, but Martin will be there with you both, blessing you with his love. And even more wonderful is this: The time will come when you will love ALL others, all humanity and all beings, with a love that is as pure and deep as that with which you have loved Martin—nay, purer and deeper than anything you have yet known. And when that day comes, in this lifetime or any other, all Heaven and Earth will rejoice."

Twenty-Five

"As the ripples caused by a flung stone stir the surface of a whole pond,
so your joy-making shall spread in ever-widening circles, beyond all
your knowledge, all anticipation. Joy in Me. Such Joy is eternal."
-God Calling edited by A. J. Russell

With Kristen in my thoughts, I can't help thinking of my friend Janine, too. She was born into a large, traditional Greek family, and all of her siblings had long-since married by the time we met. She was 40 then and had given up hope of ever falling in love.

One night, quite unexpectedly, she met the man of her dreams. They fell madly in love and planned to marry. Janine had always seemed fairly quiet and serious to me, gracious but in a distant sort of way as though she were afraid of letting anyone in too close. But once she met Russ, all of that changed. She became a warm and happy woman who laughed easily and seemed to be in love with life itself.

Late one night she received a call, saying that her sweetheart had been killed in a motorcycle accident. One minute he was alive and racing through the night toward her; the next, he was dead and through no fault of his own.

Janine seemed to shrivel before my very eyes. She became a shadow of her former self and lost 25-30 pounds on a frame that was much too thin to begin with.

This happened years ago, but she grieves even to this day. She seldom smiles and never laughs. She's gracious and beautiful, but all the joy she once felt seems to have vanished. What about Janine, God, and others who have suffered as she has?

Yes, my dear friend Janine. She does grieve still. That's her choice, of course, not mine. I want only the best for her, yet only she can decide what the 'best' is.

Janine had for many years yearned for a loving relationship, yet she had not always been as loving to herself as she might have been. She had wished for happiness, yet she had not always nurtured the activities, relationships and ways of being that offered happiness. One must cultivate bliss if one truly desires it.

Joy is like a fountain. Unrestricted, it pours forth.

When Janine fell in love, a wave of contentment flowed in and all around her. At first she swam, bathed, reveled in it. But then fear took hold. What if this should end, she wondered. Without realizing what she was doing, she placed just the tiniest point of a finger over the spout. She'd been hurt once or twice before and thought that by stemming the flow, by holding back a little, she was protecting herself. All she was really doing was obstructing the stream of joy that could have been hers.

And then her fiancé died; and when he did, the

font stopped altogether, just as she'd feared it would. But it was not death that plugged it; it was Janine's fear, and grief, curbing the flow. It remained that way for a long time. Only when she was ready, only when she lifted her finger the slightest bit could it begin to trickle in again. Eventually, she let up still more, and the fountain streamed in. If it didn't gush, then that was only because Janine didn't let it—and doesn't let it even now.

You may say that she and others have no choice in the matter of grief. And I say to you that you have choice in everything always. Janine allowed her grief to assuage when she chose to allow it, yet she clings to a part of it even now.

Her relationship with her fiancé was a catalyst for joy. But one does not need to be in such a relationship to be happy. Happiness lies within each of you. As you cultivate those things that nurture your soul, even death itself cannot stop the font for long.

This is true for Janine, for you and for all who grieve. Will you keep your finger over the spout, or will you allow the goodness of life to flow freely? It's your choice, Janine's choice and the choice of all. Life is to be lived. How you choose to do that is up to you.

Choose joy, if you will. Or pain. Or sorrow. Only you can decide, each of you. I'll honor your choice, whatever it is, always.

Twenty-Six

"You are a child of the Universe, no less than the trees and the stars; you have a right to be here. And whether or not it is clear to you, no doubt the universe is unfolding as it should. Therefore, be at peace with God, whatever you conceive him to be. And whatever your aspirations, keep peace with your soul..."
-"Desiderata" by Max Ehrmann

And then there was Mama. She was 48 years old when my dad died. They'd been childhood sweethearts, as you know, God, had eloped at a young age and had been married 30 years by then. Dad contracted a rare form of cancer; and though Mama knew he would very likely die of this—she was 'prepared,' so to speak—she could never have guessed just how his death would affect her.

People who knew her said she was never the same after Daddy died, and within two years she was dead herself. I always felt she gave up on life and died, in a sense, of a broken heart. She tried—oh, she tried—to be happy, for her own sake and for the sake of her four children. But she withered after Daddy died, as though she didn't quite know how to keep breathing on her own.

It was difficult, of course, Pam, very difficult for her. Not only did she miss your father terribly but the financial worries coupled with the challenges of raising four teenage children on her own made it harder.

But this new life brought opportunities for her, as well. Elma was 18 when she married, a child really who'd seen almost nothing of the world. She worked hard, supporting the two of them while your father attended the university, then dental school and beyond, and also helped raise her younger brother and sisters after her own mother died. She felt the weight of many responsibilities at a very tender age.

Then she became a stay-at-home mom, raising her own beloved children and volunteering in the community. She was happy most of the time. But a part of her felt she had missed out on so much. She yearned to travel more, to get a better education, even to work again once the four of you were in school and busy with your own lives. She wished for more meaning and purpose in her life.

Of course, she was never the same after your father died. Who would be? Even the smallest of incidents causes each of you to evolve. How much more then would an event of such magnitude impact one's life?

After your father died, Elma scheduled an operation that she'd put off for a long time because of Howard's illness. The surgeon uncovered some problems that had arisen years before during one of her pregnancies and corrected them. She awoke to a thinner, trimmer, more attractive body than she'd had in years. She became a hostess in one of the casinos, and this new responsibility empowered her. She felt young again and began dancing—'twisting' into the night with you and your sister and other young people she came to know at her job. She tried on different outfits, so to speak, took on different roles, began to get to know herself in a way she'd not had time to do before. Some who knew her judged her for this. But I would say to them and to all, judge no one. Each of you must find your own path in your own way; the trail that seems right to one may seem dull or senseless to another.

The last two years of Elma's life were challenging, but they led her along a road of discovery; thus, they were important for her. Remember, you were only a young teenager then and saw things from a rather limited perspective, little knowing or understanding what your mother was feeling much of the time. She was sad, yes; but she was also excited, interested, grateful and glad at times. What a lovely woman she was! You were—are—fortunate to be her daughter!

One other thing I might just mention: Your parent's marriage lasted 30 years, concluding in this lifetime with your father's death. Your marriage has lasted 27 years, ending at least for now in 'separation' and possible divorce. The first marriage would be deemed by most as successful; the second, a failure.

But I would say this: Each was perfect, just as it was. Each afforded you, all of you, the opportunity to love, raise a family since that's what you wanted, experience joys and tribulations and discover a bit of who you are. Each was a success if it helped you to grow and become more loving human beings. The married life, the single life, the life of partners living together—one is no better or worse than another. It's your choice always.

Death—or divorce or any 'parting' of lives once joined (though I say again, there is no such thing as 'parting')—may seem to close a door; but as one door closes, or appears to, another one, a hundred portals, open. Cherish the memories of those you have loved and 'lost.' Know that your loved ones, and the love that bound you together, never dies. It, like you, lives on forevermore.

Nighttime medley...

The room is pitch black, save for the light from a crescent moon and a few stars peeking in through the bedroom window. I stand for a while, staring out at the western sky.

The spark from the match I've struck carves through the darkness, and soon the glow of candlelight softens the room. Placing the "Cosmic Waltz" onto the CD player, I pull my exercise bands from the bedpost; and my nighttime ritual begins.

This is my new exercise program, but it feels more like a meditation. Following the cadence of melody, I lift and lower, lower and lift as all my cares from the day slip away. Another unlooked-for gift from the Universe arrived just the other day when I was offered, without my even asking for it, a part in an exercise video, complete with a free trainer who comes to my home three times a week and a myriad of fitness classes to prepare for my new role.

Already a few extra pounds have dropped away, my tummy has tightened and my thighs have toned. And my mind... well, my thoughts seem to have settled a bit, too.

Expand, contract, lower, lift. The Universe narrows to this moment in this room on this night. I relax into the stretch, aware, appreciative and in awe of all that Life has offered.

I lift and lower, lower and lift. And I breathe...

Twenty-Seven

"In fearlessness and love, I spend today."
-A Course in Miracles

This morning as I listened to the news, I learned that a child has been abducted from our area, God; and, of course, the parents are inconsolable over what might be happening to her. I personally can't imagine anything worse, with so many unknowns and so many cases that are never solved. Along with the pain comes guilt, I suppose, even when the parent could have done nothing to prevent it. How does one cope with this grief and with all the other emotions that accompany such a tragedy?

Any way one can, Pam. What else? Of course, when one has a strong faith or a belief in an afterlife, that parent continues to hope, whether or not the child is ever found. He or she can assume rightly that no matter what happens during this lifetime, terrible as it may seem, it occurs for a reason. Each of you chooses your experiences, difficult as that is to understand or accept, as part of your eternal healing and your evolution toward love. And, of course, your souls live on after your earthly life, free of any pain or anguish you experience here.

But how does one survive if he or she has no such belief? How does a parent in that situation go on from day to day?

One step at a time. One moment and then another and another. One heartbeat... then two... then three. You and many others have known this emptiness, this despair in different circumstances, and you have survived and become more compassionate as a result. Your faith has helped you. Even without such faith in the safe return of the child or in a hereafter, one finds glimpses of joy. The world is black for a while for these people—utterly—yet eventually the soul finds cheer in even the simplest things: A song from one's childhood; the glitter of sunlight on a pond; a toy in a shop window that reminds the parents of the good times before the pain. The spirit is a beautiful thing, courageous and strong, reaching, ever reaching for light.

As Gandhi said, "In heaven, there are no religions, thank God!" Whether or not you, the individual, believes in me or eternity or anything else, I, Eternity, the Soul lives on; and no belief or lack thereof changes that. What IS, is. The soul inherently knows this and strives for that which is eternal— peace, joy, reverence, love. Even in agony, it seeks the pinnacle; it yearns to know Itself, to remember its identity, which is God, which is Love, which is Life

Eternal. As I've said before, even in winter, deep beneath the icy snow, verdant life flourishes.

How does one cope, you ask, and I answer, "One breath at a time and then another and another." Darkness cannot abide when even a glimmer of light shines through. Perhaps the parents will discover that the child is alive and well, after all, perhaps not. But even then, the child has not truly died, only changed form. She lives on, and her parents cannot help but know that this is true. A springtime breeze, a sparrow lighting on a window ledge, a memory, a lullaby, soft and low—all are the voice of that child speaking tenderly to its parents. Remember me, it says. Remember your Self. We will always be together. We are one, forever and ever, for all time.

Twenty-Eight

*"We must be willing to let go of the life we planned so as to have the
life that is waiting for us."*
-Joseph Campbell

With the recent kidnapping so present in my mind, God, I
can't help thinking of my own children. Twenty-some odd years
ago, as you know, I was feeling a void in my life. I prayed for a
child, and along came John David. He was so sweet, and John
and I felt so lucky to have him. And then, two years later, Will
arrived, our little red-faced bundle of joy.

My sons have meant so much to me. I consider them two of
your greatest gifts. How difficult it must be for those who can't
have children yet want so much to be parents. Why are some of
us so blessed in this way and others not?

Each person is blessed equally, though it may not
seem so, Pam. Each of you has chosen the blessings
you most need in this lifetime. Just because you desire
something does not make it the thing that is most

right for you. Sometimes it's the wanting yet not receiving that brings the greatest blessings, and learning, to all. Remember, each of you chose your life and its various challenges long before you came to earth; and in your own way, even though it may not seem so at times, you continue to choose them.

Some of you are blessed with children; others are not. But they are blessed in other ways. Sometimes it is the absence of children that causes them to reach out in much needed ways to a niece or nephew or to an orphan who longs for parents and a home. Sometimes it guides them to professions that allow them to touch even more children than they would if they'd had offspring of their own. They become teachers, pediatricians, authors of children's books, songwriters—the list goes on and on. Sometimes just the coming to terms with one's frailties or lot in life is the greatest blessing of all. As the saying goes, "Happiness does not come from having what you want but from wanting what you have." Happiness comes from within, not from without; and not from others but from yourself.

The same might be said for the parents of children with special needs. Most parents-to-be pray that the unborn child will be healthy and whole. And yet, I would say to all, pray only for that which will enable you to be your most loving self, no matter what, and pray for the vision to see the wonder and beauty within all. Those who open themselves to this find untold blessings, and few regret in the long run this opportunity that has come their way.

One need only be aware and appreciative to find

life's bounty, for it's everywhere. Love your children, Pam; be grateful for them always, for you are indeed blessed. But know, too, that even if you had not had children, at all, or if your offspring had been born with disabilities, you could have been equally as happy if only you'd decided to be.

Abundance is everywhere. Only open your heart, and you'll find it. Be joyful.

Peace to all. Blessings to all my children always!

Twenty-Nine

"It is your voice to which you listen as He speaks to you. It is your word He speaks. It is the Word of freedom and of peace, of unity of will and purpose, with no separation nor division in the single Mind of Father and of Son. In quiet, listen to your Self today and let Him tell you God has never left His Son, and you have never left your Self."
-A Course in Miracles

My children have taught me so much over the years, God. One lesson in particular stands out today.

When my older son John David was about 10, we had some difficulties—a 'parting of ways,' you might say. We both had quick tempers and were easily riled by the other. I hate to admit it, but I spanked him more than once and truly battled physically with him when he was defiant. If I could go back and change anything, my physical and verbal abuse of my son, though mild and some would say perfectly acceptable, is something I would eliminate altogether. Since I can't, I'm doing my best to forgive myself and hope John has forgiven me, as I have him.

In any case, this is what happened, and it has made all the

difference.

One morning, John David and I argued—about what, God only knows.

Yes, I do, though I won't bother to remind you.

Well, thanks. I appreciate that.

We continued to bicker until John said something I thought rude and disrespectful. At that point, I instructed him to go to his room.

"No!" he said, looking me straight in the eye. Then he turned and strode off down the street.

I watched him, open-mouthed, unable to believe what I was seeing—my 10-year-old son blatantly defying me. I thought about chasing after him, even envisioned myself tackling him, funny as that seems now. But then what would I have done? Dragged him back? Given the neighbors the unpleasant, even amusing opportunity of witnessing such a humiliating display? Even in my rage, I wasn't about to do that. I have some pride, you know!

Yes, I'm aware of that.

Oh! Well!

Anyway, getting back to my story...

For a long time, I stood where I was, trying to understand and struggling to find an answer. Inside I was trembling with fear more than anger for if my son were defying me now at such a young age, what would he be like as an adolescent? I had lost control—I could definitely see that—and I was terrified at the thought. Here I was, a teacher and a rather strict one at that who had never put up with disruptive behavior from students of any age level; and yet I could do nothing with my own child. I'd lost him.

At last, in an effort to calm down, I set off for the back yard. Kneeling, I worked away at the soil in my garden, loosening it, pulling weeds, praying.

"Help me," I whispered. "I've lost control of my son. I don't know what to do."

For a long time, I sat where I was, my mind replaying the scene and my fears surfacing and resurfacing.

'I've lost control. I've lost control completely,' I thought.

Then an odd thing happened. It's hard to describe really, except to say that a voice, a very loud and distinct voice inside my brain, spoke to me.

"Do you want control," it said, "or do you want love?"

I stopped. The voice was so clear. And then it came again. "Do you want control, Pam, or do you want love?"

I didn't hesitate.

"I want love," I answered. "I definitely want love."

It seems strange now that I could so easily give up control of a 10-year-old boy; but in that instant, I did. Peace filled my being, and I knew without doubt I'd made the right decision, the only decision I could make.

It changed everything.

Almost immediately, I felt a hand on my shoulder and looked up to see John David standing behind me. Tears stood out in his eyes.

"I'm sorry, Mom," he said.

"Oh, John." I gathered him into my arms. "I'm sorry, too, so sorry. Let's never treat each other that way again, ever. Okay?"

"Okay," he said.

And we never have.

We've had our moments, of course. But those moments have

been much more civil, and I've never considered using force of any kind to deal with them. I've watched my words, as well, knowing how damaging those can be when used as weapons to destroy rather than tools to build. We've both learned to say, "I'm sorry," right away and, "I love you," often. It has made all the difference.

Yes, and isn't it ironic, Pam? With love, one has no need for control, of others or of oneself. Where love abides, all things—and people—come together perfectly. Of course, all things—and people—are One.

Thirty

"There are no ordinary moments."
-The Way of the Peaceful Warrior by Dan Millman

My son Will has taught me many things, too. He was such a sweet little boy, so easy to get along with and so kind that I sometimes worried he was too good for this world and that something bad might happen to him at a young age. Instead of dwelling on it, though, I put it into your hands, giving thanks for this precious little gift and asking you to watch over him for me. I 'let go and let God.'

Thankfully, he lived out his childhood years quite happily. As a teenager, he's not quite so angelic, but still he's wonderful. Right now, for example, he's going out with a girl from his high school, and he's so sweet to her. Every month on their 'anniversary,' he buys her flowers, takes her out to dinner and does so many nice things for her. I've never heard him say a mean word about anyone, and he's remarkably talented and funny. I can't imagine life without him.

Then don't imagine it. If you find yourself
dwelling on the past or fearing the future, consider, if
you will, changing your thoughts and plunging
consciously into the present, this moment, this now.
Will taught you that when he was just a toddler, don't
you remember?

I'm not sure I do.

You do. It was on a rather gray day when, feeling
a little housebound, you took him outside for some
fresh air. You were several miles from home, pushing
him in his stroller, when a torrential rainstorm hit.

Oh, yes, I do remember. I turned around and raced for
home, totally oblivious to the fact that he'd managed somehow to
climb up onto his seat, wrap his chubby little arms around the
handles and fling his head back in an effort to catch the raindrops
on his tongue. When I finally noticed, I skidded to a stop and
grabbed him to keep him from falling out.

Yes, then laughing at Will and at yourself, you
tilted your face to the sky, flung your arms out and
opened your mouth as wide as could be to taste the
raindrops yourself.

Yes, and to think I'd been in such a hurry to get home and
out of the rain that I almost missed it—the mountains behind us,
the mist all around, the blurred beauty of everything drenched in
rain! It was magical!

Miss no more, Pam, as Will would tell you. Be

present every moment. See the goodness and beauty of life always.

I'll try, God.

Before we end our discussion today, though, there's one last story I'd like to tell about another lesson I learned from my son John—one that fits well, I think, with what we've discussed so far about how to move past the pain of broken relationships.

Good. Let's hear it.

John was a senior in high school at the time and wasn't seeing anyone special, having broken up several months before with his former girlfriend. She and I had remained friends. One morning, she tearfully called to tell me that her date for prom had unexpectedly 'put the moves' on her the night before and, when she resisted, had canceled their prom date set for that very night. She had bought an expensive dress for the occasion and had been looking so forward to it after a year filled with pain following the breakup with John and her parents' difficult and unexpected divorce. She was wondering, she said hesitantly, if I thought John would be willing to take her.

John wasn't home at the time, and I knew he'd written off prom since he'd gone the year before and didn't really want to spend the money. Nevertheless, I encouraged her to call back later, if inclined, to ask him herself.

"Well, maybe," she murmured, the pain evident in her voice. "I'm just not sure I'll get up the nerve."

When I ran into John a little later at a high school baseball game, I told him about the call, about his friend's ordeal the night before and about her date's refusal to accompany her to prom.

"I can't believe he'd do that," John said, then eyed me

suspiciously. "She wants me to take her, doesn't she?"

I nodded, insisting that he should do whatever he wanted and that in no way should he feel pressure from me, if she called, to say yes.

When the game ended, I returned home and was folding clothes in the laundry room when John walked in and withdrew to his bedroom, which is next to the laundry room, as you know. This afforded me the unexpected, though not unwelcome, opportunity of eavesdropping on his phone conversation—thank heavens!

You're welcome.

Ha! Very funny!

"Hi," I heard him say. "This is John. I just got back from the baseball game, and..."

The small talk continued. Finally, he came to the point. "Well, anyway, what I called about is... I know this is last minute and all, but... I was wondering if you don't already have a date for tonight, if you'd like to go to prom with me."

He paused. "Okay... well, good! I don't have a tux or anything, but I can wear my black suit. And I was thinking we could go to that restaurant you like so much for dinner before the dance and... What's that? No way. I'm paying for everything. I've already bought your corsage, so I was hoping you'd say yes."

He was lying about the corsage, of course, but it was a white lie. So please don't hold it against him—okay, God?

Wouldn't dream of it!

Thanks.

Anyway, going to prom wasn't necessarily what John had

expected or wanted to do that night, but he did it anyway and had a good time. And the thing I loved most about it was that he didn't wait for his former girlfriend to call him. He took the initiative himself, relieving her of the burden and offering her a little miracle at a time when she needed it most. Needless to say, that was one of my proudest moments as a mom. And it was definitely his way of helping her move past her pain for a night, at least.

My kids have taught me many lessons over the years, God, and so have you. Thank you for it all and for the miracle of life itself.

Thirty-One

"Be impeccable with your word. Speak with integrity. Say only what you mean. Avoid using the word to speak against yourself or to gossip about others. Use the power of your word in the directions of truth and love."
-<u>The Four Agreements</u> by Don Miguel Ruiz

Now that I'm dating again, God, I'd like to ask you about some things that have been bothering me. First, since I'm still legally married—and since we haven't even talked about getting a divorce yet—should I be going out with other men? John's been seeing other women, I know, so it seems fair that I get on with my life, too. But what do you think about all this?

Second, all of my dates, so far, have been on a strictly friendly basis with nothing more than a goodnight kiss, a holding of hands or a quick hug. But what worries me is this: Since I still love John, I feel like I'm deceiving the men I date. I've told several of them the truth, that I just want to be friends and that I still care for John. For some reason, though, I'm not comfortable telling others, especially a few that I think really care for me. I feel like I'm writing a Dear Abby letter here, but I don't know what to do about this. It's all so new. Will you help me?

Dearest one, ask me anything at any time. I'll help you in any way I can, so long as it's never at the cost of your free will.

You're doing nothing wrong, so you don't need to be bothered by the fact that you're dating now. You and your husband have parted ways for the time being, and you know he's been seeing others. He seems to believe this is perfectly all right, so naturally he must think it's fine for you to go out, as well. He often drops by when you're not at home, and you haven't been available many times when he's called, so naturally he must assume you're out with others.

As for the men you're seeing, you've been quite open whenever they've asked about your marriage and sometimes even when they haven't. It's true that one man in particular may not know how you feel, but notice that he has purposely avoided the subject. Perhaps he doesn't want to know; perhaps he thinks in time that your relationship with him will naturally become more intimate—or not. On the other hand, since you're bothered by this lack of communication, perhaps you ought to openly address the subject so you'll again have peace of mind. That's of utmost importance, isn't it? Only you can decide how best to accomplish this.

The important thing is that you must trust yourself and others to do what's right. You'll know when it's time to go into more detail. Speak your word impeccably. You owe yourself and others that. Be honest, but also be open to the possibility of love and romance if it should come along. Give the best you can to all you meet, no matter what. You'll never regret it.

Your biggest fear, I think, is that you feel it's not fair to be your best self if that means someone may fall in love with you and get hurt. That's a consideration, certainly. However, remember this. Not only must you trust yourself to do and say what's right, what's honest and true, and to be your best self, but you must also trust others to be able to take care of themselves. If you were professing love for another, yet secretly not feeling that love, your lies could, of course, cause harm. If, however, you continue to be open and honest with the men you're seeing and with everyone else, for that matter, you have nothing to fear. Love everyone, see the goodness in everyone and be your kindest and best self always. Help each person you encounter to see the perfection in himself, as well. Then, no matter what happens in the future, even if you part ways with that person, you will have been true to yourself and true to your brother, giving him the best you could and helping him to see the good that lies within you both. Your relationship will have left him better off than before, for he will have learned about love, love of himself and love of all. And so will you.

Thirty-Two

"To love another person is to see the face of God."
-Les Miserables by Victor Hugo

Here's another question for you, God. What if, now that I'm dating, I fall in love and want to express my love for that person sexually? Should I wait until I'm married to him—and divorced from John—as I've always been taught? Or should I do what feels natural when the time comes, if it ever does?

I've given you and all beings freedom of choice, Pam, with some guidelines, of course—the Ten Commandments, for one, and others, as well, to help individuals within a society live cooperatively and happily together. Since most decisions ultimately lead to happiness or unhappiness, choose well. But as I've said before, there is no such thing as sin. I've given you free agency, not just sometimes but always. You get to decide; only you know what's right for you.

The bottom line is this: Honor your Self and love

your Self and All Creation in the most magnificent way possible. Listen to your Higher Self, which reveals the path to happiness always.

But why would you stay married to John if you've fallen in love with someone else? You probably wouldn't, so perhaps this issue will not arise.

But what do *you*, GOD, say is right or moral or ethical about this? What do YOU say?

I say, "Love the Lord your God with all your heart, might, mind and strength, and love others as your Self—AND love your Self well." Why? Because Love creates happiness. How you express that love is up to you. The question of whether or not you should be sexually intimate with another is one only you can answer. Would this make you happy, truly happy, you might ask. Right now you have a difficult time even kissing another if you're not in love with him. And yet, I say, kiss another if you're so inclined; hug, hold hands, smile, see God and your Self in all. As for your having sex, that's not about me. I have no feelings about it one way or another. It's about you, about each individual, about what your heart's telling you. Ultimately, it's about what brings you joy.

But don't misunderstand me. Choose always, if you will, that which will bring you and others lasting happiness, not necessarily that which will bring you only a moment's satisfaction or which will cause conflicts later on. I know you well. You would not enjoy sex with anyone you don't care about deeply. That's fine. However, I would say this to you, Pam:

Practice 'making love' to everyone in ways that are not necessarily sexual. Smile more. Praise. Say thank you in words and gestures. Hold hands more. Touch more. Love more. Laugh more. Be your most lovable Self always with no fear about the past or future. If you do this, you'll have no regrets.

LOVE. LOVE. LOVE. And the world will love you—and all creation—in return. Always there is a rippling effect with this. Only as you offer love to the world do you bring Heaven to Earth in this and every moment, in this and every day...

...forever and ever. Amen.

Me, again...

...only not the married me or, at least, not the 'married-but-living-alone-and-pining-for-my-husband'—or 'pining-as-much-for-my-husband'—me any more. It feels strange being 'single' again and going out on dates. But it's exciting, too.

It's like I'm a teenage girl, getting ready for my first date every time I go out and feeling all the jitters of that girl as I fix my makeup, style my hair, restyle it, dress, change, change again, primp and polish and primp some more until the doorbell rings and I have no choice but to traipse down the stairs and answer it. It's a little stressful, I must say. But fun!

Funny, too, that I go to all this trouble when the last thing I really want right now is to fall into another relationship since I'm not completely over—okay, since I'm not even close to being over—my last 27-year relationship called marriage.

But still it feels good to have men asking me out. I'm beginning to feel like a woman again, an attractive, desirable woman, something I haven't felt in a long time.

And it's good being around men again. That was a huge void in my life after John left, the absence of the adult male. I like being around men; I always have, and not just because of the romantic component. I like the relaxed I-don't-give-a-damn-what-you-think-of-me attitude that so many of them display. I like the fact that they don't seem to judge or criticize or gossip so much. Or maybe they do, but I haven't seen that side of the men I've come to know, and I like that.

I'm not one to sit around with my lady friends, spreading rumors or telling male-put-down jokes. I love being with a friend, male or female, and having a deep, intimate conversation about the things that matter to us. I love that! But as for sitting around making small talk, I don't get it. I just get bored.

Anyway I'm glad to be dating again, even if I'm not exactly a pro at it. You forget after 27 years even how to flirt.

Just the other night at a TGIF, for example, a very good-looking male acquaintance asked if I'd like to get a bite to eat.

"Oh, I ate before I came," I said artlessly, "and promised my dogs I'd take them for a walk." I was just being honest.

"My dog could use an outing, too," he persisted. "How about if we have dinner first and then take the dogs out together?"

It was then I realized he was asking me out. So we had a bite to eat and walked our dogs. It was nice.

At another TGIF, a man I'd recently met asked if I wanted to go to a movie that night.

"No, thanks. I've heard it's violent," I replied without hesitation.

"Could I call you tomorrow then?" he asked, cupping his hands in a gesture of begging. "Please?"

"Me?" I blurted out before I could stop myself. Clueless, clumsy, anything but what a sophisticated woman would say.

Oh well. It's been a while...

Still, I'm having fun as I try on my new role of 'single-and-going-out-again.' It's been almost 30 years since I hung that outfit up in a closet and forgot all about it. Now I've taken it out again, brushed it off and tried it on. It still fits, though it's a bit tight in places and a bit uncomfortable. Those, I suspect, will relax in time. I've hung a different outfit, my married one, in that dark closet now. I've closed the doors, though not too tightly, and I haven't locked them yet.

In a few hours, I'll be going out with my new friend who asked if he could call. I'll give it an hour or two to see if we engage in meaningful conversation and have anything in common, at all. Or maybe I'll even stretch it to three.

We'll have to see...

Thirty-Three

*"Wherefore take unto you the whole armor of God, that ye may be able
to withstand in the evil day, and having done all, to stand."*
-Ephesians 6:13

Last night I had the strangest dream, God. Oddly enough, I
wasn't myself in the dream but rather a little boy of about six or
seven with dark hair and an olive complexion. I've never before
dreamt I was someone else, and yet I very clearly felt I was that
little boy experiencing everything that happened in the dream.
And it all seemed so real.

I, as this little boy, lived in a small town during the late
1930's or early 40's. Off in the distance, I could see a train ready
to depart; and I knew that inside, pressed together in one of the
cars, lay my family. The reason I knew this was because I
remembered another time when my family and I had huddled
together, shivering and hungry, on that same train. In fact, this
dream felt as though it were a repeat performance of an earlier
experience but with one major difference: This time I had a
choice as to how I would play it out.

It was late at night, and I was hurrying to a lighted building several blocks from the station, hoping to find some food for us. All the while, I dreaded going back because I knew that if I boarded the train, I would die. Nevertheless, stronger than any sense of danger was my love of my family and my desire to be with them in their hour of need. And so I hurried on.

Surprisingly, the workers in a makeshift cafeteria, where I found myself, allowed me to heap great helpings of leftover meats—fish, chicken, pork, beef—onto a platter. A thought occurred to me that I shouldn't mix meats in this way, that it might not be healthy; but realizing I had very little time, I piled them on, then hurried out the door with the heavy plate of food in my arms and began racing toward the train.

Already, the first cars had begun to move. Many people outside the train were shouting and struggling to open the boxcar doors, trying, I suppose, to free the prisoners inside or to climb aboard themselves to be with their loved ones. Flames, flashes of light, loud explosions filled the air, while guards whipped at the mob and drove them away. All the while, I raced on, clinging to the huge platter of meat, praying I could reach the last car before the doors slammed shut.

I was too late. Still holding the heavy dish, I stood helplessly by, watching as the train steamed off into the night

At last, finding an abandoned truck by the side of the road, I climbed in and slumped against the back seat. Before I could close the door, two huge dogs jumped in beside me. They snuggled against me, keeping me warm as I closed my eyes and fell into a deep, dreamless sleep.

The next morning, I awoke to the sound of voices. Opening my eyes, I saw a throng of townsfolk peering in at me through the car windows. They were smiling and pointing.

"Look," one of them said. "What a cute little boy! And see

how the dogs have kept him warm through the night. He must have been left behind when the others were taken away."

They were friendly faces, and I knew they had come to help. At that instant, I awoke.

Two things stand out as I reflect upon this dream: First, in my attempt to save others, I saved myself; second, all of us were connected—the animals that sacrificed themselves, willingly or not, to give us nourishment; the dogs that nestled against me, keeping me warm; the victims on the train and those of us outside, willing to die rather than abandon our loved ones; the townsfolk, in the end, who came to save me.

It was a sad dream but beautiful, with a message of love and hope. What do you have to say about it, God? It seemed so real, and I felt so much that I *was* that boy who'd been inside that train before, in this or another lifetime.

You'll find lessons in everything, Pam. Dreams, whether they reflect reality or not, can be tools for healing. Your observations about this dream are right on the mark.

All of humanity and all of creation are one—one with me, Creator of All. Taken symbolically, the victims trapped inside the train are but the shadows of your own fears. Whether or not you were ever on that train in this or another lifetime is not important; what is important, if you wish to be free, is that in this lifetime you face your fears, all fears, while wielding the weapons of love, compassion and courage. In your dream, you did this, as did the others who were trying to reach their loved ones, even at the cost of their own lives.

As you loved the victims inside that boxcar, love

yourself, all of yourself, even the shadowy, fearful parts. Observe yourself as though from afar, an objective witness, who notes, "Ah, there she goes again. There goes Pam, cringing before her fears, which are simply shadows, insubstantial and illusory." And then, recognizing this in yourself, choose peace. Free yourself from fear, for if you but denounce it, it will dissolve before your eyes.

In your dream, you felt and acknowledged your fears, but you did not let them stop you from rushing to those you loved—no, not for a moment. And though you arrived too late—it's never too late, by the way, since your mere intention is always enough to bring healing and help—still you ran on through the night, carrying your heavy burden, refusing to lay it down no matter how tired you became.

It's been said that courage, like a muscle, must be exercised. And exercise you did in this dream. Fear is but a word. Erase it. For though its imprint may remain, it will become more and more indistinct with each erasure until it is hardly discernible at all.

These next several months will be a time of trial for you, Pam. You'll be coming to a crossroad, and you'll have to decide which path to tread. Remember this dream, and be courageous. Choose the path of peace, inner peace, and truth, whatever you decide that to be. You'll never regret it—no, not for a single instant. This time is important for you, a turning point, no less. I will be with you through it all. You have so often prayed to attain the energy levels of peace, joy, love and even bliss in this lifetime. Keep these goals in mind as you make your choices.

Do you see how beautiful that young boy was as he sped through the darkness with his heavy platter, as he ran with joy and even peace despite the exploding guns and mortar fire all around him, despite the death he could smell in the air and feel in the cargo of the train? You are that boy. You carry the same beauty, Pam; you must see that. It's important that you see it. Only then can you see the beauty that is in all others. As you recognize this in yourself, you'll find the courage to open your heart. Once you do that, you will never again hold back. You will be all you are and all you want to be—now, in this lifetime.

Race through the night, Pam, for the light is just over the horizon, hidden for the moment but there, always there. And I will run with you, every step of the way, for I love you. Oh, yes, dear one, I do love you—you and all of your brothers and sisters, all beings, all Creation—so very much!

Thirty-Four

"I have learned in whatsoever state I am, therewith to be content."
-Philippians 4:11

Except for my sons, I'm not sure I've ever really known how to love completely. Maybe I'm just too caught up in myself. With all my heart, I'd like to find someone who can love me—and I, him—in a way beyond anything either of us has experienced; and someone who will join me in trying to make a positive difference in the world. Will I ever find that kind of love, God? Is it I who prevents that kind of intimacy with another?

Look at your words, Pam. "I'm too caught up in myself," you say. Quite the contrary, I'd answer. The fact is you don't love yourself enough, which is why you can't love another in the way you want. If you loved yourself more, you'd naturally attract love and be able express yourself and that love without inhibition or restraint. You'd show the true YOU always.

Yes, but here's the other problem, God: I'm never satisfied. Even when I was happily married, there were times before the kids came along when I felt restless and unfulfilled, as though I had not yet met my true love. Instead of seeing my life with John as perfect or, at least, sufficiently happy, I kept feeling there should be something more to our marriage, that maybe I'd settled for less romance and excitement than I wanted and deserved—and that maybe John had, too. It wasn't as though we had nothing in common; we had everything in common, or most everything anyway, and John was my best friend. I loved him deeply.

The trouble was, I wanted more.

A common refrain, wouldn't you say, Pam?

Yes, God, I admit that. I'm trying to do better, but... well, it's hard to break old habits. I am working on it, though.

I'm not judging this, Pam. I'm simply observing.

Well, it's true; and I'm sure it's contributed hugely to my unhappiness or, at least, my disquiet over the years.

Anyway, I think it was during one of my college English courses that I first read Plato's *Symposium*. In this, as I'm sure you know, the playwright Aristophanes spins a tale about why humans are always restlessly seeking their other half. Supposedly in the beginning, humans were once either male, female or androgynous, each with two heads, four arms, four legs, two sets of genitals, etc.—in other words, sufficient and complete in and of themselves. Unfortunately, in this perfect state, they became proud and began threatening the gods until Zeus, never one to put up with such pride for long, raised his thunderbolt and literally sliced the people in two. And now each of us goes through life, seeking our other half yet seldom able to find just the right one.

I guess that's how I sometimes felt in my marriage to John— that I'd found a wonderful man, a kind and handsome and exceptionally bright and capable husband, just not my other half.

So I think a part of me was always searching for... something different, always assuming that other people had found what they were seeking and that I needed to find that, too. If I'd only stopped to observe my friends and family more closely, I might have realized that each of them had their own set of challenges every bit as complicated as the ones John and I faced, and that relationships do, in fact, as the saying goes, take work, hard work.

But I didn't realize it. I just knew that though my marriage was good, it wasn't perfect—and I wanted it to be perfect. I wanted a husband and lover and spiritual partner, all in one, not just a husband and good friend. I wanted a soul mate.

Maybe John did, too.

Anyway here I am, still searching for that soul mate, wondering if maybe I just didn't recognize him when we were together—or wondering if he's still out there somewhere, looking for me, too. Am I being too idealistic, God? Will I ever be satisfied? Or will I go on seeking something or someone that couldn't possibly exist?

> Seek no more, Pam, outside yourself, if you seek
> peace and perfection; seek only that which is within.
> Be in love with every moment and with all creation.
> Don't worry so much about whether or not you've
> found your 'soul mate.' All are soul mates in their own
> way. Whether you knew it or not, whether you felt it

or not, John was indeed a soul mate, despite—or perhaps because of—his ability to take you out of your comfort zone at times. Maybe he wasn't the most romantic husband always; but in his own way, he demonstrated his love for you and his sons over and over, as did you for him and for them. Neither of you was particularly adept at expressing your feelings through words and affection, yet each of you managed to say, "I love you," over and over most days, in your gifts of thoughtfulness and support, in your willingness to listen and help one another and in your many acts of kindness.

Still, the two of you have come to this impasse; and though you may think you've somehow failed in your marriage and in life, you have not. Your relationship has changed, that's all, and perhaps this transposition is not so bad as you might think. Is it not allowing each of you to explore new avenues and new relationships and certainly yourselves in a way that would never have occurred otherwise? Is it not causing you to look at what is, just as it is, with a new kind of acceptance and grace?

Reach out to all with love and empathy. As you do, you'll inevitably attract, like a magnet, those who approach life as you do, your 'soul mates,' as you say— though I repeat, all beings are soul mates. Send love out into the world, and the universe will respond with love for you.

Therefore, be your most joyous, peaceful and loving Self. Then, no matter what, you will find the 'soul mate' within, and you will be happy for you will have discovered something greater than anyone or anything outside your Self could give. You will have found the true and authentic You, which is Me, which is Joy, which is Love at its best.

And truly, what more could you or anyone else want?

Thirty-Five

"Lord, let me honor myself this day. Let me be... kinder, gentler, friendlier... not to please anyone, but just to say I am that I am..."
−<u>Science of Mind</u> *November 2001*

No questions for me today, my dear? And yet, you look so sad.

Sit down a moment, and breathe in. Gaze about you, opening your heart a little as you do, and look again. Be patient. True peace and intimacy comes when you are open to all, when you can look beyond to that which is invisible to the world.

Say often the words from Isaiah: "This is the refreshing." This-is-the-refreshing. Let the words bring perfect peace. Relax. Breathe them in. Live them. Love. And know that all is well.

Relish the silence, even in your sorrow. Let it seep into your soul and find its source. As a newly fertilized egg propels itself forward, then plants itself firmly along the lining of the uterus to grow, develop and become, so, too, will your inner peace find its place within you. It, too, will grow, develop and become.

And you will heal; indeed, you've already begun.

Thirty-Six

"Today I whisper softly, "Namaste," to those I meet. It is my personal blessing as we pass upon the streets of life. Your presence is a reminder that we are one. Namaste, my sister, my brother; it's no mistake that we met. It's my opportunity to express the perfect God in me as I greet your face of God."
-Science of Mind Sept. 2001

Here's another question for you, God: Why do so many people have trouble being their most loving and authentic selves? Why is it so difficult at times to show warmth and affection, even to those we love most?

Somewhere along the way, I began putting an emotional distance between others and myself. As a teenager and especially after my parents died, I thought it was 'cool' to be a little aloof, to reserve my smiles, to put up a facade of not caring too much. When my children were small, of course, it seemed natural to hug and kiss and hold them. And even now, I think they like it when I rub their backs or kiss them good night.

But with others, I tend to be a bit shy, so though I'm often the first to greet them with a cheerful hello, I have a hard time becoming really close. I often fail to look people in the eye or smile broadly at them or laugh out loud. I'm hesitant to sing along to the radio when I'm with others even when they're doing so, though my voice isn't that bad. I'm self-conscious about dancing, even though I've taken lessons and have had plenty of compliments from dance partners over the years. This reticence takes some of the joy out of life, and I'd like to overcome it. I'm sure others would, too. Could you help us to be, simply and authentically, our true selves?

Think of that moment not so very long ago, Pam, when you sat in the assisted care dining room with your father-in-law who was once so wise and articulate but who appeared then confused and old. It seemed difficult at times to communicate with him; he could hardly hear you when you spoke, and he so often seemed in a different world altogether. And yet, somehow in that moment you were able to remember who you really were and, in doing so, you saw past the illusion of age and decay to who he really was, too. You forgot about the small talk and sent love to him, to his authentic self, to his soul, and you knew that somehow you'd connected. You saw it in his eyes and in his voice and in the way he relaxed and smiled and became animated as he told you his latest story. You communicated from your heart and gained intimacy on the deepest level.

Strive for that with all whose paths you cross. Send them love, and let your soul commune with theirs. Bless them with this thought: "Namaste, my brothers and sisters. I honor that which is in You and in Me and in all Creation, that which is divine and eternal, that which connects each of us to one another and to God."

Relax. Surrender. Above all, be fully in the moment. Be-fully-in-the-Now. Slow down. Notice. Take the time to look into another's eyes. Speak tenderly. All creation is filled with longing for just such a soft word, a smile, a gentle touch. Be aware and appreciative of all.

Sometimes you cannot think of a single word to say. Say nothing at all. Only be there, aware and appreciative of that moment that is unique among all others, a gift, an opportunity to express Love, which is You and Me and all Creation. Don't worry so much about whether or not you're fulfilling some promise within this lifetime. If only you love, you're fulfilling it. You, Pam, are an educator and an author, yet one kind word could be more valuable to someone else— to yourself—than a thousand words on a page or in a classroom. One never knows how much one small gesture can change a life.

"I would see you as my friend, that I may remember you are part of me and come to know myself." So says *A Course in Miracles*. Make this your goal today: Observe yourself, as from a distant star. Stay focused. And listen. The starlings in the nearby trees are ecstatic with song even though it's winter and the ground is covered with snow. Tonight the temperatures will plummet, but the birds don't fear. They're singing their hearts out in joy for what exists right now. The sun shines down on them and on you. The sky is a deep and azure blue. Your son has come home to write a college paper and to be with you. Your dog lies by your side as you write these words that I—God—whisper to you. Someone in this world—nay, many—love you very much, and all is right on this earth, right here and right now.

So smile and dance and laugh. Sing your heart out. If you're a little off key, no matter—some of the most famous singers of your day sing 'off key,' and it's this uniqueness that sells their music.

You have much to offer the world, Pam, as does everyone, each of my children, all beings. Do not hold back, any of you. Be your Self, and the world will be a better place for your having lived.

I love you....

Thirty-Seven

"Today belongs to love. Let me not fear."
-A Course in Miracles

It's Saturday night, God, and here I am, home early from a party—my choice, I know—and feeling once again, even after all this time, the emptiness of a broken marriage. I keep asking myself how it could ever have come to this. I wasn't supposed to separate from my husband; I wasn't supposed to be here alone tonight or any night. And yet, here I am, sitting by the fire with my two dogs, feeling very much alone.

As I've said before many times, Pam, you're never alone. You know that, do you not? Even now, this night, angels sit beside you, stroking your hair, whispering to you, bringing you comfort and help. They love you, as do I, as do your children, as do all of your brothers and sisters. Give this time, Pam. Be patient.

I cannot say what John will do, for only he can

decide. But I can tell you this. He does love you, in his own way. Tonight he, too, feels a kind of emptiness, a longing for what might have been, for what could be. Trust. Trust John. Trust the Universe. Trust Me. Trust your Self. All is as it should be, now and always.

Be still. Be at peace. All is well.

Remembering…

It was a line-up. I wanted to attend a sorority party, but my 'true love' was in Missouri. John had scheduled a dinner party with his fraternity buddies and their dates, but his 'true love' was off traveling around the country. A mutual friend brought us together that night.

The doorbell rang, and I tromped down the stairs and rounded the corner to find a cute, hippy-looking blond with blue eyes and hair down to his shoulders. He held a single red rose in his hand.

Not bad, I thought. Still, he won't be a problem for Dick and me.

To be honest, I was relieved; I didn't want anyone or anything getting in the way of my plans to marry Dick some day.

I relaxed, accepted the rose and set off on what proved to be one of the more memorable nights of my life. I loved this guy's sense of humor, his relaxed style, the delicious dinner he cooked for his friends and me. We didn't finish in time to make it to my sorority party, but it didn't matter.

I was glad when he asked me out again—and when he brought yet another rose, and another, and another.

It took many dates before he kissed me and many more

before he told me he hoped "I wouldn't mind," but he thought he was falling in love with me. As it turned out, by the time he finally said those words, I found I didn't mind a bit.

But soon after that came Dick's big fraternity party at the University of Missouri. Dick knew I'd been going out; he'd been seeing others, too. But he knew nothing about John, since up until about a week before the trip I hadn't seen any reason to tell him. Even as I packed, I felt a growing excitement to see Dick again.

It wasn't until I was seated on the plane and lifting off for Missouri that I realized suddenly I didn't want to be there on that plane, that the only place I wanted to be was back home with John, the man with whom I was falling in love. The man I eventually married.

Still remembering...

I could see him perfectly from my second-floor bedroom window, smacking the tennis ball again and again against the wall of his fraternity house across the street from where I lived.

Things were going well between us.

We still laughed about our first date, which our mutual friend Ann had arranged, but not before warning John that though she thought we'd have fun, she doubted that I'd ever be his 'true love.'

"How rude!" I'd laughed when he told me. But secretly I'd thought, 'It doesn't matter because you won't be my true love either. Dick already is.'

Of course, that was before my disastrous weekend in Missouri when I'd confessed to Dick that I'd begun to care for John. Essentially, Dick and I had spent the weekend arguing, and I'd left on Sunday, eager to resume my life in Utah and to see John again.

"Dick called you 'Toilet,'" I told John as I admitted to him where I'd been over the last few days.

He thought for a while about what I'd just disclosed to him and then relaxed and laughed. "With a name like that," he said, "Dick ought to be more careful."

Those days were sweet. But looking back now, I can't help thinking Ann's words were more prophetic than any of us realized. I'm certainly not John's true love now, and I wonder sometimes if I ever really was.

But maybe I was. We did, after all, have so many good times...

Starlit ski outings under a full moon, floating along on the snow, carrying hot wine in a leather pouch and Gouda cheese and a loaf of bread in a backpack, laughing, reciting Frost's "Snowy Woods" and marveling at the beauty of the sky, the trees, each other.

Backpacking in the Uintas, driving up after work and camping under a moonlit sky. Sipping hot coffee and munching cinnamon buns at dawn, traipsing up the trail to Four Lakes Basin and swinging in our hammocks long before most hikers had even begun their trek.

Lounging in front of the TV, eating gigantic helpings of pizza in celebration of our mountain conquest after each backpacking trip.

Running with our three dogs at dawn along Guardsman Pass near Park City, then celebrating that night with people watching, burritos and beer at Utah Coal and Lumber, our favorite Mexican restaurant.

Traipsing home after an evening out, laughing delightedly at the snowflakes drifting down around us.

Gazing out at the world from the tops of mountain peaks after an all-day autumn climb, then gorging on steak and fries and dancing at our favorite bar near Cottonwood Canyon.

Backcountry skiing with a picnic lunch, our dogs racing beside us down powdery slopes on another beautiful day in paradise.

Transforming with love and labor our 100-year-old miner's house from an old shack to a beautiful cottage.

Biking through Yellowstone, alternately camping out under the stars and luxuriating in all the famous, old-time lodges.

Setting out on car trips with the family to Lake Louise, Mesa Verde, Santa Fe, Dallas, Disneyland, Las Vegas, Jackson, Yellowstone and beyond, ever assuring little John and Will that the car would surely "go faster" if only they'd stretch out their chubby arms and rub their tired parents' heads from the back seat.

Celebrating life with relatives, friends and neighbors—and sharing so many happy times with dear Nam and Gamp.

Chatting by the fire with John Denver playing in the background, sipping wine and exchanging stories; or collapsing on the deck after a hard day's work, savoring the joys of just being together.

So many memories—good times, for sure. I think we must indeed have been in love.

No matter what happens, I'm thankful for my life, for all that was, for all that is and for all that ever shall be.

It's good to reflect, not with sadness over what I've lost—since as my dear Friend says, one can never really *lose* anything—but with gratitude for all I have. And I have, have always had, so very much!

Thirty-Eight

"As you come to seek and see the virtues and strengths and nobilities of others, you begin to seek and see them in yourself, also. As you draw to yourself the highest currents of each situation, you radiate that frequency of consciousness and change the situation. You become more and more and more consciously a being of Light."
—<u>The Seat of the Soul</u> by Gary Zukav

As I walked to work today, God, I thought about many of the things we've talked about, and a picture began to form in my mind.

As I understand it, every event, situation, circumstance and relationship is perfect for the healing each of us seeks in this lifetime. And as we heal ourselves, we bring emotional and spiritual health to our brothers and sisters and to all creation, as well.

Right, so far?

Right, my child; go on.

Well, this is what came to me: Each of our experiences is like a baby left on our doorstep. We can embrace it while it's in our care, or we can resist it, walk around it and ignore it, though it cries out to us for love. If we neglect it, the child will intensify its wailing until we're forced, at the very least, to notice it. If ever we truly want peace and quiet, we'll pick it up and nourish it. Then and only then will the cries cease; then and only then will we, in a sense, be free. On the other hand, if we flee from it, we might escape the wailing for a while; but the memory will follow us everywhere, haunting us until at last we return, lift the infant into our arms and tend to its needs.

The child might be beautiful and bright. Or it might homely, deformed, damaged. Even then—perhaps especially then—it needs care, love and nourishment. As we resist it, we're merely postponing the inevitable—more and more babies placed on our doorstep, more wailing, more hunger, more need, more discontent. But when we embrace it, healing comes at last, to the infant and to us all.

How eloquently you've put this, Pam. Yes, cherish each moment, if you will, the beautiful and the difficult, for every circumstance is a blessing and an opportunity to remember who you are and who you forever want to be.

If you find yourself resisting, you might ask what it is in that moment that you fear, for that's the child crying out to you. As you honor it, cradle it, lift it up into your arms and accept it with joy and compassion, you'll move past the pain and see the possibilities, the beauty and the gifts of healing.

Yes, I see that now, and I think I finally understand. I'm

looking at my child, this infant that's been placed on my doorstep; and I'm picking it up at last.

I see that John may not be coming back, ever, certainly not in this lifetime. It's hard, but I do embrace this situation, accept it and give thanks. Let me resist no longer but instead find the gifts, all of them, and be glad.

And God, at times I may forget to be as loving to this child as I want to be. Please, if I forget, remind me.

And thank you, my Friend, thank you so *very much* for helping me finally to see.

Thirty-Nine

"Today the peace of God envelops me, And I forget all things except His Love."
-A Course in Miracles

How beautiful it is, God, walking with you now out under an evening sky. Thanks for the fresh snow blanketing the earth and for the blue sky and sunshine that has blessed this day.

Tonight I'll go to bed early, putting all my problems on hold, placing them in your hands if you don't mind and then crawling in beside them as I drift off to sleep.

Yes, leave your cares with me tonight, Pam. Tomorrow when you awaken, you'll find all the answers you seek. They're inside you now, just waiting for the key of inner peace to unlock them. We'll work on them together.

For now, sleep, rest and know that all is well.

Sweet dreams, my child. And peace.

Forty

"Judgment and love are opposites. From one come all the sorrows of the world. But from the other comes the peace of God Himself."
-A Course in Miracles

A woman I recently met called me last night, God. She was despondent and desperate. Apparently she's fallen in love with a man she's been seeing for the last six months. She felt he loved her, too, since he had assured her of that and had even mentioned marriage. They've been sexually intimate until a few days ago when she discovered he was engaged to another woman. I don't know why she called me, but she did.

"I feel so stupid," she said, her voice tight with pain.

Hesitating, I searched my heart for an answer.

"Don't," I said at last. "You did nothing wrong. You merely loved him, and there's nothing stupid about that. The worst part, I think, is not that you unknowingly fell for a man who was engaged to someone else or even that he was able to deceive you in the way he did, but that he didn't love himself enough to be true to you, his fiancé or himself. Now that's stupid—or sad anyway."

My message seemed to help. Thanks for giving me the words.

> Yes, but remember this, too, Pam: Don't judge this man. Judge no one, for the workings of the heart are beyond human understanding. Forgive all—this man, yourself and all others—and see through all appearances to that which *is*. Look past all perceived faults to find the beauty of the perfect soul of this man and of all others, souls that I created and that are one with me. As one of your heroes, Mother Teresa, said, "If you judge people, you have no time to love them."
>
> You're on a journey, each of you, and you'll all make mistakes at times. Nevertheless, know that all is as it should be—with this despairing young woman, with this man, with you and with all. Trust and love. My words, your words, brought healing last night. Know that each person involved chose the lesson that each needed. Trust. Love. And know that all is well.

Forty-One

"If, as Scripture says, 'God is love,' then human freedom is real. As Dostoyevsky's Grand Inquisitor properly discerned, freedom is a burden, choice is scary. But freedom is the absolutely necessary precondition of love. We are not slaves but children of our Father, free to do good, free to sin. So when in anguish over any human violence done to innocent victims, we ask of God, 'How could you let that happen?' it's well to remember that God at that very moment is asking the exact same question of us."
-Credo by William Sloane Coffin

This morning as I was hiking up Iron Mountain, I remembered the Robert Frost poem, "Stopping by Woods on a Snowy Evening." Just for fun, I added a refrain to it. It fits with my new goal of being more present. Want to hear it, God?

Of course. Go ahead.

Okay. First, here's the last stanza of the original poem:

The woods are lovely, dark and deep.

But I have promises to keep,
And miles to go before I sleep,
And miles to go before I sleep.

And here's my addition:

And yet, this Now I'll hold and keep,
The forest dark, the woods so deep.
Because this Now is all that's mine.
This Now, and this—oh, shine, oh, shine!
Divine.

I kind of like it. What do you think?

I like it, too. It has a good message, one to remember.

Yes, and I needed it tonight as I listened to the 6:00 o'clock evening news full of shootings, wars and all manner of senseless violence. I'm afraid I didn't exactly stay in the now as I thought about all the people and other creatures in the world dealing with this insanity. Will we ever learn, God?

The world may seem to be in a state of turmoil, Pam, and certainly many, especially those who have not yet evolved spiritually, do choose to use violence in their dealings with others. And yet, just look about you and see the faces of good, decent people everywhere who do the best they can to help others and lead happy lives. Far more good exists than evil, far more beauty than horror, far more love than hate.

Perhaps instead of listening to the news and

focusing on what's 'wrong' with the world, you'd be happier doing what you did this morning, walking outside, looking about you and breathing in the cool, refreshing air of the universe. Watch the birds as they dart ecstatically through the skies, smell the fragrance of pine and woods and let those simple pleasures nurture your soul. As you do, you'll discover the peace that resides within all life forms—inside you and all beings—awaiting only your awareness of it now, always now.

But, God, really! What about all the crazy people who go into shopping malls, theaters, schools, even their own homes and, with cold-blooded premeditation, shoot to kill anyone in their path? It makes no sense. It's just plain evil. You say you love everyone and everything and want the best for us, so how can you condone or even forgive this sort of behavior? It couldn't possibly be the best, could it? And if you're everywhere, then that means you're with the killer, too, as he shoots his victims. I don't get it. I just don't get it.

Perhaps you want me to say that I don't love the killer quite as much as I love the rest of you or that I don't love the killer at all. If so, I'm afraid I'll have to disappoint you, Pam. I assure you, I love everyone equally every single instant of every single day throughout eternity. I am Love. Love is all I know. Ultimately, Love is all there is.

That isn't to say I condone the violent acts of the killer or that I don't writhe in agony with those who lie on the ground, bleeding or dying. Or, for that matter, that I don't feel the hellish torment, the low self-esteem, the anguish and despair that drove the killer to kill. I do; I feel it all. As my children suffer, I suffer. But I rejoice, as well, for I am Love—and so are they, the killer and the killed. Each will live past this moment and the next, past all apparent suffering and loss. Each of you is a personality while on this earth, but you are a soul forever.

Eternal life involves eternal progression. Every situation, every instant, every act, violent or not, becomes an opportunity to heal, evolve and love; every event allows you to align your personality, and all of its frailties, with your unlimited and beautiful soul. It may not happen in this lifetime, or the next, or the next. But it WILL happen.

Let me ask you this, Pam. If one of your sons murdered someone, would you abandon him? Or would you not love him anyway and try to help him if you could? Even if you were sickened by the very act, even if you were heartbroken and filled with black despair, would you not try to understand in some small way why he was driven to such a deed? I think you would.

And so do I, for I know that despite the apparent hatred, insanity and heartlessness of the individual— the personality that is the killer—the soul lives on. And that soul is Love. Eventually, in this lifetime or another, the tormented will seek peace, happiness and forgiveness. It is the only way.

The energy of love is powerful indeed; it neutralizes the negative forces that you read so much about in newspapers and tabloids. Whether or not this is clear to you, it is true. So, love. Love all. Perhaps in another lifetime, you were the murderer who had not yet discovered compassion or love in her heart for others—you who cannot bear to harm even a mosquito during this lifetime. Pray for all; love all. As one individual loves, so, too, does another, and then another, and another... until, like the flame from one candle to many, joy lights the world.

I love you, no matter what you do, say, think or feel; I will always love you, you and all your brothers and sisters, all creation equally. Peace. Peace. Amen and Peace.

Forty-Two

"I used to think I knew how some caterpillars become butterflies... I
figured if I were to cut open a cocoon, I'd find a butterfly-ish
caterpillar, or a caterpillar-ish butterfly, depending on how far things
had progressed. I was wrong. In fact, the first thing caterpillars do in
their cocoons is shed their skins, leaving a soft, rubbery chrysalis. If you
were to look inside the cocoon early on, you'd find nothing but a puddle
of glop. But in that glop are certain cells, called imago cells, that
contain the DNA-coded instructions for turning bug soup into a
delicate, winged creature, the angel of the dead caterpillar."
-Martha Beck O Magazine *January 2004*

Okay, God, I get it. No matter what, your message is simply
to love everyone and everything—murderers, sexual predators,
assassins, neighbors, friends, family members and ourselves.
Easier said than done, in some instances. But I'm listening, and
I'll try. I promise.

I'm also attempting to focus more consciously on the
present—not brooding about the past or worrying about the
future—but once again I'm having a hard time because I just
learned of a huge earthquake in a small country far away across

the ocean that has left death and devastation everywhere. So many in that area are homeless, hungry and freezing in winter temperatures without adequate shelter or help. And, of course, most are grief-stricken over the loss of loved ones and virtually everything they've ever owned.

I've heard your words, and I believe them, God. But still I can't help but grieve for all who are going through this pain.

> Grieve if you must for now, Pam. Hopefully, the time will come when you'll grieve no more, for you'll see the perfection in all things, in all events, in all creation. In everyone's life, trouble strikes or seems to. Yet, in reality, all is well.

> Remember the caterpillar. Just as it spins its cocoon and immerses itself in blackness, so all, too, at times will dip into darkness and despair. But have patience. Trust. Believe. For inside the cocoon, transformation begins. As you, all of you—those in the earthquake-torn country and those everywhere else—surrender to your experiences and let go of all that holds you back, you like the caterpillar-turned-butterfly will metamorphose into your most beautiful state, a state of compassion and beauty that you might never have experienced otherwise.

> Detach from the outcome, and surrender to all that is right now. Of what matter is it how you eventually emerge from this moment—as a leopard-spotted butterfly or as a monarch? Each is exquisite, and each has a purpose and role on this earth.

> Those who now suffer in this devastated area of the world chose this life, and they will choose their deaths, as well. Do what you can to help them. Send

money and supplies, if you will, pray for them and bless them with your love. But also trust and know that I am God and that all is well. They may suffer now, but out of the darkness comes the opportunity for rebirth, for newfound peace, for freedom and joy. And, of course, no matter what, their souls live on, continuing to seek their wholeness, which is, of course, here within them all along.

Grieve if you must, when you must, but know that outside the dark cocoon in which you may now reside is a radiant world of eternality and light. Be patient, defenseless, open to the miracle of healing and rebirth that is going on all the time. Each moment—each 'tragedy'—embodies the most wondrous possibilities. Look past what appears to be to what *is*, to whatever you want that is in keeping with the highest good for all. You have asked for love, joy, peace and enlightenment. It is yours. Only trust. Love. And find ways to bring peace and joy to the world.

Forty-Three

"Heaven is the decision I must make. I make it now, and will not change my mind, because it is the only thing I want."
-A Course in Miracles

I have another question for you today, God. Do heaven and hell exist, as so many religions claim? If so, what are they really like?

My child, there is certainly a heaven, and it begins with you. Let me ask you this: Are you passionate about life? Do you love others and yourself? Do you spend time doing what makes you happy? Are you peaceful, and is life a joyful adventure, full of purpose and meaning? If so, what greater gift than these can exist? And what more perfect heaven?

As for hell, there is only that which you have manufactured in your own heart and mind. It is not the eternal fires of the damned, as so many religions have purported; it is not part of an afterlife. It's part of *this* life. Simply put, hell is unhappiness, and unhappiness is hell; and both are descendants of morose, unloving thoughts. It was not I who fabricated this torment for you. I do not judge; I do not condemn. And I certainly do not send my beloved children to a world of despair. Who then did? You, my children, only you with every choice for sorrow that you have ever made. You can, of course, choose otherwise, if only you will.

"Beyond this world there is a world I want." So says *A Course in Miracles*, and so say I. What do you seek, my children? What kind of life—heaven or hell?

No matter what, know that I love you always.

Heaven or hell—hmm, interesting...

John and I created both in our marriage, as I suspect most every couple does at some point.

Perhaps if there'd been a law compelling married couples and partners to enroll periodically in a relationship class or support group, we might have seen we were actually doing quite well with the whole marriage thing. We might have relaxed more and enjoyed the challenge that comes with any relationship—AND been more alert to the pitfalls.

But like so many others, we didn't see the need to take action until it was too late.

The first several years of our marriage were pretty smooth. We backpacked and skied and worked on our house and ran with our dogs and did so many things together that we had little time to get bored or antsy. But then I, for one, began to feel an emptiness inside and a compelling desire for something more— more romance, more passion and, above all, a family of our very own. John wasn't sure he was ready for that, and so the void and restlessness increased.

As a result, I had several emotional affairs, all very innocent sexually but a reflection, I think, of a very definite shift in our marriage.

Once, for example, when I was in my late 20s and off skiing by myself, I rode up on a lift with a man who was visiting from California. We instantly bonded. We spent that day and the next skiing, laughing, relishing the little time we had together. When we finally said good-bye at the end of the second day, he asked if he could kiss me. I said no since I'd been forthright from the beginning about my marriage and also open with John about my new ski partner, but a part of me wished I could say yes. We never wrote or saw each other after that, never even exchanged addresses; but I didn't forget him.

Then, several years later, I took a biology class taught by a university professor who was extremely charismatic. After our last class, he invited me to lunch and asked if I would consider having a relationship with him, insisting that if we were careful, we wouldn't hurt either of our marriages. I refused, though I must admit I was deeply attracted to him and fantasized for months about a possible affair.

Fortunately, by the time he contacted me again to ask if I'd like to conduct some field research for him and be co-author of a paper, I was happily pregnant with my first child and not at all tempted to so much as impart the tip of my toe through that door. My restlessness ceased, and the nine-month period that followed was such a sweet time for John and me, a time of intimacy and dreams and a deep and abiding tenderness. Heaven itself!

Parenthood brought with it its own set of challenges; and more often than not, at the end of the day, we'd fall into bed, too exhausted to say, "Amen," much less make love. Needless to say, our romance suffered.

And yet the years passed in relative contentment and ease. Family bonds took over, and our date nights became family nights, perhaps to the detriment of our intimacy. John and I chatted over coffee in the mornings and relaxed together in the evenings after the boys were asleep; but our conversations became more and more centered on our pets and children than anything else, and our lives together passed in amiable aloofness.

We tried, though; I think we both wanted desperately to reconnect. We often took walks together, just the two of us; we skied together, with the children and without. We hiked on occasion and did some of the pre-kid activities that had once been such an important bond. We held hands, addressed each other with terms of affection and certainly supported one another in most every way. But we had lost much of the physical intimacy that we once enjoyed. A crack formed, almost imperceptible at first; then a deepening fissure, and finally an ever-eroding crevasse.

One night as 1 lay in bed, watching John sleep beside me, I felt as though a great rift as deep and wide as the darkest ocean had settled between us. I yearned to bridge that gulf, but I didn't know how and wasn't courageous enough to risk rejection.

Twenty-five years into marriage—29 years into the relationship—we admitted near-defeat and contacted a marriage counselor. We both worked hard to be honest, to listen and to mend our wounds. But the bottom line was this: We'd lost our romance years before, and now we were losing our friendship. We didn't seem to have as much fun together as we once had or the slightest inkling—'no idea in hell'—of what to do about it. We tried; we really did. But it was like giving a terminally ill patient medicine to keep him alive when really you knew he might be better off dead.

Finally, in a last-ditch effort, we decided to separate. Naively, I thought it would help us rediscover our love for one another, but John apparently didn't see it that way. Once apart, he seemed happy to be free and single and dating again. And I...

I was devastated. I hadn't expected it to end like that; in truth, I hadn't expected it to end, at all.

Despite my restlessness over the years, despite our differences, I actually felt that as marriages go, we had a pretty good one. Many couples with far more problems, and worse ones, stay together for a lifetime.

For some reason, John and I just couldn't do that, couldn't keep hanging on to a raft that, no matter how many times we blew puffs of air into it, seemed destined to sink.

One might argue that we just didn't hold on long enough, that help was on its way. And maybe they'd be right...

But maybe they wouldn't.

Maybe what really happened, much as I've hated to admit it to myself, was that we loved each other and ourselves enough to let go. Maybe each of us instinctively knew that by loosening our hold and drifting off by ourselves, we'd both have a chance to survive.

The truth is, sometimes you've just got to know when to let go. Sometimes, even when you feel like hanging on forever, you have... to... force... your... fingers... open... Otherwise, everyone goes down with the ship.

And sometimes... sometimes... by letting go, you finally learn to swim.

Forty-Four

"The Universe is the result of the Self-Contemplation of God. Our lives are the result of our self-contemplations, and are peopled with the personification of our thoughts and ideas."
-The Science of Mind by Ernest Holmes

Over the last several months, you've asked me many questions, Pam. Now I have one for you. What exactly do you want in this lifetime, now and in the future? Your present circumstances are the result of choices you've so far made. Some are to your liking; others are not. Some you produced consciously and blissfully; others you welded through fear. *But you created them all!*

What if I were to tell you that you could have anything you want *right now?*

I'd love it!

Well, you can. If you want happiness, make the

choices that bring you joy.

That's exactly what I want, in this lifetime and forever. How do I do that, God?

All is energy and light, Pam. Look inside. What are you feeling right now? Rapture? Sadness? Fear? Love?

Quite honestly—and I hate to admit this since it seems awfully irreverent when I'm talking to you, God—I'm not feeling much of anything, at all.

Then change that. Feel joy if that's what you want in your life because what you're feeling *is* important. You're the producer of every event, every relationship and every instant of your life. Truly. *YOU are the creator.* So perhaps it would be well to design your masterpiece consciously.

All that you have engendered in the past has led to this moment right now; all that you embody now— every thought, word and action—will impregnate your future.

But I thought you were the creator, God.

I co-create through you, but ultimately I've given you the freedom and ability to mold your life here on earth and throughout eternity. In my love for you and all beings, I've blessed you with the power of creation. You're connected to the energy of the universe—to me and thus to the very same energy with which I create at all times. Powerful, loving, joy-filled thoughts and feelings attract powerful, loving, joy-filled events. Fear-filled thoughts breed fearful events.

I've definitely experienced that! Several years ago, after a stressful day at work when one thing after another seemed to go wrong, I left the building upset and out of sorts and immediately got into a fender-bender when a student, distracted by a phone call, backed out of a parking place without looking behind her. Within that same hour, as I was running errands, a mirror flew out of the back of a pickup truck. It smashed on the road directly in front of me, and a million tiny pieces of glass flew up and pitted my car. I was shocked and incredulous and ready to cry.

Your negative energy attracted other negative energy—do you see that, Pam?

I didn't then, but I do now.

The opposite can happen, too, of course.

Yes, I remember a time when it did...

Tell me.

When John and I were first married, we bought a hundred-year-old, very rundown miner's house and fixed it up so that it was cozy and cute.

You were happy then.

Very happy. One day, as we were driving around a new part

of town, we noticed a beautiful house with flowers on the front deck and aspen trees all around. We fell in love with it—our dream home, we called it—though clearly it was way beyond our means.

Ten years later, with two boys and three dogs underfoot, John and I began searching for a bigger house. We made an offer on one, only to find that the listing agent had outbid us. Several months passed with no affordable or desirable place in sight. In desperation, I turned to you.

Next time don't wait so long

I won't. I promise!

Then I relaxed, feeling in my heart that everything would work out perfectly, and it did. The very next week, our real estate agent called to say that the owner of one of her favorite houses in the Park Meadows area had just lowered the price by $30,000. We drove over to take a look, and there it was—our dream home, the exact same one we'd seen and loved ten years earlier! I still live in my dream cottage today.

It makes me happy just to think of it.

It should. It was what you wanted, what you chose—with joy.

Choose with joy always. Or not. It's your...

...I know. It's my choice, right?

Always! You're the artist of your life. The peace, joy and light—or the darkness and sorrow—that you weave today become the threads and fabric for tomorrow.

Choose well, my dear, my children all. And know
that I love you…

… always.

Forty-Five

"Teach only love, for that is what you are."
-A Course in Miracles

The other day, I experienced a moment of enlightenment as a teacher, God. Sam, a student in one of my high school English classes, has been driving me crazy. He seems so cynical and so judgmental of me and of his peers. Though he's obviously intelligent, he's lazy, never putting forth much effort and earning only a C in an honors class that requires a B or better. In short, I came to the conclusion that he probably ought to transfer to a regular English class, and I was looking forward to saying good-bye.

But then one day, as I was thinking, "If I let him stay, maybe he'll change," I heard another voice (was it Yours?) saying, "Sam isn't the one who needs to change; you are. Change your perspective, and accept him for who he is." In that moment, it was suddenly clear to me that I, not Sam, was the one with the problem. I needed to value him as a person, just as he is, and to realize that whatever I disliked in him, I probably disliked in myself.

The next day, as he marched down the hall toward my classroom, I stopped him. Holding out my hand, I said, "Sam, we've gotten off to a bad start this year, and I want to change that. I've judged you unfairly. I suspect you're a great person, and I want to get to know you better. Friends?"

We shook hands, Sam with a shocked look on his face and I with a smile on mine. Sam was kind to his classmates and to me that day. He was courteous and polite. And even when he made a few of his usual caustic comments, I wasn't the least bit bothered by them. My acceptance of Sam allowed me to lighten up and enjoy him for the good person he is. It has made all the difference. Thank you for reminding me.

Forgiveness, the opening up to the beauty of each soul, illuminates the most amazing truths. How little effort it takes to love another. When you do, you discover that you love yourself, too.

Forty-Six

"I love the recklessness of faith. First you leap, and then you grow wings."
—Credo by William Sloane Coffin

God, I'm beginning to think that I'd like to make a change in my profession. I've loved teaching, but lately I feel I'm ready to retire and do something else, yet there are so many unknowns and what-ifs. What if I can't make ends meet in retirement? What if I regret my decision and want to return, only to find there are no openings? How can I best fulfill my long-term goal of positively impacting the world? Is there something else I should be doing, something that would make me happier and allow me to spend more time with you and those I love? I have so many questions and no definitive answers.

Be at peace, my daughter, and trust. Meditate, sit quietly and take long walks out in nature. As you discover your true self and listen more intently to your higher voice, you'll find answers to all your questions.

Moment by moment, day by day, they will all come together like the pieces of a jigsaw puzzle.

Trust. Trust me, your spirit guides and your Self. If you feel you should take this step, you must. Everything points to this. Only fear makes you hesitate.

Or does it? Perhaps you have something left to do in the classroom; perhaps that's why you have not left. You seem to love it. Listen to your heart, and follow it, wherever it takes you.

Well, I have to admit, God—and I'm sure this comes as no surprise to you—I'm a bit of a control freak in my classroom. This works well for classroom management, and I do think most of my students learn tons each year, as a result. But I can't help feeling that if I could relax more, joke with them more, get to know them better as individuals and not just as students, I'd have a more profound effect upon their lives. Until I can learn to do that, I guess I'm not ready to move on to other things.

Then don't. Not yet, at least. Again, Pam, I say to you, "Follow your heart." There are so many ways one can impact the world. If you enjoy teaching, and if you feel it challenges you to become more authentically the real You, then stay with it. But do all you can to be the person you want to be, inside the classroom and out. Many years ago, I asked you a question when you and your son were in conflict. Today I ask it again...

Do you want control, Pam, or do you want love? What will it be? Control in your classroom and out? Or love?

I want love, God, just as I did so long ago. I definitely want love.

Then give love today, tomorrow, the day after.
Love and be lovable always. The rest will follow.

Okay, God. From this day forth, I give up control—or try to—and choose love. Only love. It's going to be challenging after all these years.

The classroom is a microcosm of your life, Pam. As you send love to your students and colleagues, you send love to all. In all things, spread peace, joy, love and light into the world. Then, no matter what, you'll be happy.

Step forward, unafraid, trusting that the universe will hold and sustain you, whatever you decide for your present or future career. Treat this as you treat all of life's decisions, as a great adventure, an opportunity to make a difference in the universe. Your dreams will unfold; your wishes will come true.

Be not afraid. All is well. Believe this, for it is so.

Forty-Seven

"Don't take anything personally. Nothing others do is because of you.
What others say and do is a projection of their own reality, their own
dream. When you are immune to the opinions and actions of others,
you won't be the victim of needless suffering."
-The Four Agreements by Don Miguel Ruiz

A week has passed since my informational meeting with
students who were thinking about signing up for the next Europe
trip I'll be leading, God. At first I wasn't going to take on another
one because the last one seemed too good to be true, and I didn't
think I'd ever be able to match it. Besides, I thought traveling
every two years like this hurt my marriage, so I had intended to
give it up.

But with John no longer in the picture, I've decided to go
ahead. It will be good, I think, to have something else to think
about for a change.

The meeting was packed full of students and parents who'd
heard good things about the last trip. And now, one week later,
we have almost half of our deposits already in. It's unheard of!

Miracles occur when you allow them to, Pam, as we've discussed. You create your life, all of it, though at times you may not think you do. I suggest you see always what you want, no matter whether it appears, as yet, or not. Visualize your dreams, believe they're coming and detach from the outcome, realizing that what you truly desire is simply the best and most harmonious good for all. In this way, you surrender the final outcome to—and create with—the blessedness and perfection of the Universe itself.

Yes, but now some new complications have set in, God. One of my colleagues who runs a competitive student trip recently learned that many students have signed up for my trip, while only a handful have so far signed up for his. He's stepped up his recruitment efforts, which is fine, except that he seems to feel it's perfectly okay to enlist students who have already signed up for my trip. He's also accused me of things that just aren't true and has attacked my trip to others and, now that I've confronted him, to me. I feel his actions are unethical and fear-based. I've told him this, and we've talked and smoothed things over a little.

But who knows what he'll do or say next. No matter what, I don't want to be infected by his venom. Help me, Father. When someone attacks me in this way, how should I respond?

First, my dear, take nothing personally. This is about your colleague and his perceptions, which are only that—perceptions and apparently misguided ones, at that—and not about you or your trip. Nothing other people do or say is because of you; it is because of that which lies within them.

The same is true of you, of course, and all of the reactions you may have toward your colleague or anyone else. Your judgments about him or others don't in any way define the people you judge; they simply reflect your own thoughts and perhaps your need to critique at times.

You say you don't want to be infected by his venom, and I say to you, "Then don't be." Remember the Buddha's question: "If someone offers you a gift, and you choose not to accept that gift, to whom does the gift belong?"

Graciously but firmly refuse to take your colleague's—or anyone else's—gifts of anger and criticism. Leave them with him. However, go one step further. Pray for this brother, and send him the gift of your blessings and love. He's a good man; you know that. He's demonstrated this on many occasions. Be sure always to offer him and all others compassion and understanding, for giving and receiving are one in truth.

Be empathetic. Your colleague is hurt by what seems to be treachery on the part of his students and you. Bless him that he might realize it is not treachery at all, that it has nothing to do with him or his trip— which, in fact, will be a great success. Your blessings of peace will perhaps help him to see this in time. At the very least, they'll prevent his anger from infecting you. As you bless him, you open your own heart and bless yourself.

Nothing anyone does or says can harm you unless you allow it. If you revere your colleague, despite his apparent animosity toward you, you not only maintain inner peace but also continue the greatest love affair of all, the love affair with yourself and, therefore, with all of your brothers and sisters, all fellow beings and me.

I love you, my daughter. Love all. Love me.

Forty-Eight

"Patience and timing... everything comes when it must come. A life cannot be rushed, cannot be worked on a schedule as so many people want it to be. We must accept what comes to us at a given time, and not ask for more. But life is endless, so we never die; we were never really born. We just pass through different phases. There is no end. Humans have many dimensions. But time is not as we see time, but rather in lessons that are learned."
-Many Lives, Many Masters by Brian Weiss

I had another disturbing dream last night, God, and it certainly touched on the theme of separation, though in a very unusual way. Once again, I was someone else, a young boy, different, I think, from the boy in the other dream I told you about. I was anxious for my parents to come home because I had a piano recital that afternoon and was afraid I'd be late. I was also nervous about the recital but knew I had to go because my teacher was counting on me.

My parents finally arrived home, but my mother (not my mother in this lifetime) was irritable and edgy. I had the sense that these parents were not very caring or involved in my life, that they were rather neglectful. When I reminded my mother about the recital, she grew angry and informed me that we were going somewhere else later that day and would not be attending the recital.

My dream then jumped ahead a few hours. I had apparently run off to find an elderly man whom I had befriended and in whom I had found comfort in the past. I trusted him completely and thought he would help me.

To my horror, he took me to an old shack and began to sexually abuse me. I wrenched away from him and stumbled out onto his porch, screaming, crying out to his neighbors, who were working nearby, to help me; but they pretended not to hear. I sensed they were too afraid of the old man to get involved, though I implored them again and again until the old man caught hold of me and dragged me back inside.

Once again, the dream jumped ahead in time. Suddenly I was no longer the young boy but an observer, standing next to the mother, who had obviously become concerned about her son. We watched as the child stumbled out of a bathroom, holding his stomach and retching, then falling to the floor and writhing in pain. I sensed that the old man had literally torn the boy apart. At that moment, the dream ended.

What does it mean, God? Was this a glimpse of reality, another lifetime perhaps, or was it just a horrible nightmare? And why was I in the body of the young boy? It seemed so real.

It's not important whether this was a dream or the memory of a previous lifetime, Pam. What is important is that for some reason your mind has gone to this place for healing. Let's look at it.

Like the young boy, you have trusted people who have seemingly abused that trust and hurt you. And like the young boy, you have experienced great pain, especially during these last two years, when you have felt at times as though you were literally torn in two.

How will you respond to the heartache of external circumstances that are an inevitable part of one's life? Will you curl up into a tight ball and close yourself off from the world? Or will you venture forth with determination and courage, unwilling to allow anyone or anything, any life event, to prevent you from truly living—and loving—with joy?

Each experience affords you the opportunity to face your fears and heal. I'll help you. Trust, for you've survived much in this lifetime, and every other, and have grown all the more compassionate because of it all. Learn from every incident, and take from each the gifts of love, peace, joy and light. Then offer them to the world, for what you give becomes your own.

Learn from this dream and from all of life's circumstances. Whether you know it or not, you have created much of the misery in your past. Create joy now, if you will. Create love. Create light.

Be open. Fill your mind, heart and soul with the possibility of all things, for there—and everywhere— you'll find me.

Forty-Nine

"I want to know if you can see beauty, even when it's not pretty, every day, and if you can source your own life from its presence."
-*The Invitation* by Oriah Mountain Dreamer

I ran this morning along a frozen mountain trail, Father. The wind whipped about me, and the air was icy cold. Little patches of snow stood out on the ground, and hoarfrost covered the sage and pine. I was chilled clear through to the bone.

But I sped on, and soon I was so warm and toasty, I pulled off my jacket and tied it around my waist. Then off I went, the sun on my back and the wind in my hair. And I, alive and free!

Yes, and I ran with you all the way.

Your morning runs are like life, Pam. At times, the trail is rocky and steep, the temperature frigid, the wind wild and every step an effort. At other times, all comes easily. The air is cool and fresh, the path smooth. Yet each step—and every experience—no matter how hard or easy, is a blessing, for each works the heart, lungs, body, mind and spirit equally, one no more or less than another.

Race on with the wind in your hair and the sunshine on your back, through green meadows and gray mist. Every moment of life is wondrous! See the goodness in it all.

Choices, choices…

Lately I've been giving some thought to my choices in life, since that seems to be a major theme in so many of God's messages.

"Choose happiness if that's what you want," he keeps saying. "Choose peace. Choose love."

But how exactly do you do that, I keep wondering. How do you just choose those things? It sounds way too simplistic—or impossible—I'm not sure which.

I do believe the quote God mentioned earlier about true happiness, that it "comes not from having what you want but from wanting what you have"—and I DO have most everything I'd wish for already. I want good things and good people in my life, and I have them. But maybe, if I really did have the choice, I'd opt for a little something more.

Take love, for example. I want love, and I have love, the love of my sons and my family and friends. I'm grateful for that and so very blessed. But I'd like the other kind of love, too, the romantic, happily-ever-after kind. And I CHOOSE that, yet every circumstance in my life tells me I can't have it for now. I'm separated from a husband who no longer wants to be married, and I haven't yet found a partner who's right for me.

But according to God, I can choose love or anything else any time I want—like now, for instance. Right now.

So, here goes…

"Dear Universe, I want love, true love. I choose true love, right here and right now…"

I shut my eyes and visualize the two of us, my partner and myself, holding hands, smiling, talking long into the night about anything and everything, working together, playing, hiking, dancing, skiing through snowy woods… and I feel all warm and cozy inside at the thought. I feel happy as I picture this.

Keeping my eyes closed, I wait…

And wait…

And wait some more…

Then taking a deep breath, I open my eyes and look around; and, of course, I see nothing but what I saw before. I'm happy anyway

Where *is* he, this future partner, this man I could love, I wonder. Somewhere, I suppose, if he really does exist, but not here and not now.

But maybe he could be, very soon. Or maybe this sort of thing takes time. I do know that I don't want to waste any more time waiting—for anyone or anything. I want to use my time, all of it, whether it's a month or a year or forever, discovering more about my Self and others and this life on earth. I'm content, more than content, with or without a partner or a husband or even a best friend (though I DO have that). I don't want to jump from one relationship to another, searching for some quick fix or someone to fill a void. From now on, I'll fill my own voids, thank you!

Anyway I could ask more questions about this choosing-whatever-you-want thing. I do, after all, have the ultimate authority at my beck and call.

Wow! I do. Like everyone else, I have the ultimate authority available any time I want; and I say I can't choose? I've chosen the most amazing thing possible; I've chosen to talk to, and learn from, God Himself!

Okay, I feel a little sheepish all of a sudden, and I'd probably feel a little ashamed, too, except that my expert wouldn't like that. He'd tell me to get over it, to love and be kind to myself, to choose forgiveness, which, according to him, means seeing the perfection in all things, even in *me*. He'd tell me he's with me, no matter what; and he is. He'd tell me to be happy, to choose joy if that's what I want. And I do want that.

So I will—and I do. I choose forgiveness. I choose joy. I choose peace. I choose love—the love of my children, my family, my friends, my future partner, if he exists, and myself.

And *voilà*! It's here. It's all here, whether I can see it now or not. All I have to do is what I'm doing right now—believe and be happy and appreciative, and then just sit back and let all the Good of the Universe come to me and all the Good inside me flow out to it and to everyone and everything.

All of that goodness *is* on its way; I know it. In fact, it's already here, in the unformed, creative stuff of the universe. Pretty soon, it will manifest in whatever way it should.

In the meantime, I choose to be happy with life just as it is, and I give thanks for the many blessings that sweep in and around me every single day, every single moment of every single hour of every single day. This 'alone' time has given me so many gifts that I honestly wouldn't trade for anything, not even for my marriage to John or for a future marriage or for anything else. It's brought me to where I am right now, and I'm grateful for that, for it all, for even the darkest of times.

Hmm. Maybe it's not such a hard thing to do, after all, this deliberate choosing of life's experiences and of happiness itself.

You just close your eyes, smile, see it happening, be grateful and then let it all begin...

...Because it already has begun, even before you—or I—ever uttered the words. Maybe even before we ever even consciously thought them.

Fifty

"Dear Lord,

"So far today, God, I haven't gossiped, lost my temper, been greedy, grumpy, nasty, selfish and over indulgent. I'm really glad about that.

"But in a few minutes, God, I'm going to be getting out of bed, and from then on, I'm probably going to need a lot more help.

"Amen."

–Author Unknown

My sister-in-law discovered the above quote in a beauty salon and gave me a copy of it, God. I like it. If you ask me, it pretty much says it all.

Thanks for being there for us even when, despite our best intentions, we fail miserably to be the good and noble beings we'd like to be.

I love you for loving us anyway.

No worries, as they say! Your best is good enough

for me, Pam. And your worst, for the most part, is just plain entertaining. (I *do* love a good laugh, you know.)

As long as your little foibles harm no one, they merely cast my children in an all the more lovable and beguiling light. I *am* the doting parent, you know.

I love you all. Always.

Fifty-One

*"What things soever ye desire, when ye pray, believe that ye receive
them, and ye shall have them."*
-Mark 11:24

Almost seven months have passed since we first began
conversing like this, God, and it's been well over a year since John
moved out. So much has happened in that time, and especially
during this last month, as I'm sure you know.

Thank you for my new friend who's so attentive and so full
of kind and admiring words. He makes me feel all glowy inside.
He seems far too intelligent, too handsome and too perfect to be
true. But it doesn't matter. I'm not expecting love or marriage
with him, nor am I nervous or head-over-heels, or anything; I'm
just comfortable and happy. Thank you for that part, too.

You're welcome, Pam, but truly you created this
for yourself. Or, more accurately, I co-created this
with you—through you. You asked, believed and
received. I merely obliged. All the universe moves to

help you when you set forth a clear enough request, you know, and when that appeal—or affirmation, rather—is charged with faith.

Relax and enjoy this new relationship. Be your true and best Self, my dear daughter, and see beauty everywhere—in this man, in all you know and, yes, in *you*, too, for it's there. Beauty is everywhere if you only open your eyes and heart to it.

My blessings flow out to you and all my children. I love you.

Love all...

Fifty-Two

"Love is patient; love is kind; love is not envious or boastful or arrogant or rude. It does not insist on its own way; it is not irritable or resentful; it does not rejoice in wrongdoing, but rejoices in the truth. It bears all things, believes all things, hopes all things, endures all things. Love never ends...
-1 Corinthians 13:1-13

Wow! Things have moved so quickly in this relationship, God. My new friend is an amazing person and seems to think I am, too. I like his company, especially his cute sense of humor, and we have a nice combination of fun and romance. I must admit, I do look forward to being with him; in fact, lately I've a hard time thinking of anything else.

But the last thing I want is to fall into the all-too-common trap of immersing myself in this to the point of distraction; I want to focus on the NOW, appreciating each and every moment, with or without my friend. I have so many important projects and people in my life right now, and this relationship is only one of them.

Please help me to find a way to stay centered, God.

Whether in a new relationship, a new situation or anything else, you have no reason to be anything but relaxed, Pam—and 'centered.' Enjoy each moment, if you will, and trust your Self to do whatever is right in this and in all things. I suggest vigilance in maintaining a proper balance each day of mental, physical, emotional, social and spiritual activities. Consciously do those things that nurture your soul, and check in with your Self often to be sure this relationship is adding to your life in some important way. You're fortunate to have other projects and people to consider. Perhaps you'll want to focus on these even more.

You've asked to be open to love. Here it is, for now. Love this man, love all others and love yourself. Love all creation and all the world! With love comes peace; with peace, joy; with joy, enlightenment; with enlightenment, God.

And it all begins again...

... With Love

...And with you, my children, *all* of you!

Fifty-Three

"Laughter has something in it in common with the ancient winds of faith and inspiration; it unfreezes pride and unwinds secrecy; it makes men forget themselves in the presence of something greater than themselves; something that they cannot resist."
-G. K. Chesterton

What a lovely day I've had, God, with your light shining down on me and everyone else—a chat with an elderly neighbor as she worked in her garden, your hands helping her dig and plant. A ride over mountain passes with the wind in my hair and a darling man beside me—and you, smiling down on us.

A hike up to a crystal clear lake, the sunshine—you—a yellow glimmer from above. A party with friends, new and old, and you, laughing beside us. Another ride, Mr. Toad's wild ride, for sure—your hand holding and steadying us, keeping us safe, your joy lifting us all the way.

A phone call from my best friend—more laughter, warmth, love—and you. A hilarious musical, the songs ringing out, touching my heart, the jokes brightening my soul—another friend, and you, sitting beside us, sharing it all.

Sleep, blessed sleep enveloping me. And you, kissing me goodnight, watching over the world and me.

Thank you for a most blessed day.

> You're welcome, Pam. And yet in many other places, rape, abuse, war and hatred all took place today—and I was there, too, comforting and holding each and every being. I am with my children in laughter and in tears and in everything in-between. See me in all, and know that I am with you and all creation always.

Fifty-Four

"It is like a Mother, who is setting aside suitable gifts for her daughter's wedding before Love even has come into the daughter's life.

"The Anticipatory Love of God is a thing mortals seldom realize. Dwell on this thought. Dismiss from your minds the thought of a grudging God, who had to be petitioned with sighs and tears and much speaking before reluctantly He loosed the desired treasures. Man's thoughts of Me need revolutionizing.

"Try and see a Mother preparing birthday or Christmas delights for her child—the while her Mother-heart sings: "Will she not love that? How she will love this!" and anticipates the rapture of her child, her own heart full of the most tender joy. Where did the Mother learn all this preparation—joy? From Me—a faint echo this of My preparation—joy.

"Try to see this as plans unfold of My preparing. It means much to Me to be understood, and the understanding of Me will bring great joy to you."
-God Calling   Edited by A. J. Russell

Help me to find peace in all that's happening in my life, God—this new and unexpected relationship. Intimacy. Joy.

And now, a whole new complication, with his children so much a part of his life, consuming his thoughts, his energy and his time and leaving so little left over for me.

Help me to understand this and to know how best to stay grounded and to be grateful for all that is. Teach me. Guide me. Show me, please, whatever it is I need to know.

Trust. You possess everything you need to handle this and all of life's challenges, Pam. Thankfulness is the key, of course, along with inner peace and joy. Only you can decide how best to achieve those ends.

Whether children are involved or not, new relationships require adjustment and effort. All is not easy. The question is, is this relationship worth the toil? Does it nurture your soul? Trust that you'll know the answer to this soon enough.

In the meantime, give thanks for the laughter, the fun and the kindness this man has shown you. But be glad for the quiet times, the hesitancy, even the distancing each of you experiences at times. It's all part of getting to know and understand each other and yourselves. It's why you 'date.'

But wouldn't you like to take time now for all the other things you love? Wouldn't that make you happier than all this worrying—if you want to 'stay grounded,' that is? Go outside perhaps and breathe in deeply, drinking in the fragrance of the earth. Wrap your arms around your sons, bury your face in the soft fur of your dogs, take a walk, say a prayer, write a poem, have dinner with a friend, smile and give thanks to all.

As you take time for those things that nourish

you in every way, you'll see how beautiful it all is—all of it, even the little complications of life. They add a bit of interest to the weave.

Fifty-Five

"Heaven means to be at one with God."
-Confucius

Last night, I saw into my friend's heart as he read poetry to me and later soothed my frightened dog, held his son in his arms and told us stories from his boyhood. I felt he shared a bit of his soul with us all, and I was deeply touched by that. Moments of intimacy mean so much to me these days; they're the times when life is sweetest and best. Thank you for all the precious instants of true connection.

Yes, share your soul whenever you can, Pam, with everyone and everything, for only then do you glimpse Heaven; only then do you discern that which is Divine, unchanging and true. As you come to know your brothers and sisters, all beings, you discover your true Self and thus Me, Love, who's there all along in all creation if only you'd take the time, each of you, to notice.

Fifty-Six

It's hard to say goodbye to those we love, God, and painful to think of moving on without them.

Yesterday my little dog Emmie Lou left me. I knew she was growing weaker and weaker, knew the time was coming when she would pass. She slept in her usual chair the night before without moving. Then yesterday morning, she could hardly open her eyes. I carried her out under the shade of an aspen grove, murmuring her name and stroking her fur, telling her how much I loved her and how wonderful it had been to share so many good times together. I read *The Prophet* by Kahlil Gibran to her throughout the day; and though she was unconscious, I felt the sound of my words comforted her.

One by one, my sons, some neighbors and my new friend dropped by to say good-bye, yet still she lingered on, though she was hardly breathing. Finally John arrived; and it wasn't until he'd said his good-byes in the late afternoon that she finally slipped away—as though she'd been waiting for him, as though she'd wanted to say farewell to the whole family and needed to feel the love from each of us before she left.

Today I'm so sad without her. Help me to understand why death must be a necessary part of all our lives.

> My Dear One,
> As I've said before, there is no death, merely a transition from one life to another. But always, always the soul lives on.
> Emmie Lou was—and is—a spirit so full of exuberance, she could hardly contain it. You remember, of course, all the times you'd take her on outings. Her nonstop barking at the beginning of each excursion was her way of expressing her joy to the world.
> "So Emmie's going for a walk," your neighbors would laugh. Her enthusiasm was contagious.
> She gave you and your family many gifts, and you reciprocated; the relationship was symbiotic indeed. Those memories will last a lifetime—many lifetimes; they're timeless. Emmie Lou is a part of you forever and you, a part of her.
> Love knows no bounds. Emmie lives on, as you must know. She spoke to you last night after she died, and her spirit hovered about you as you ran along the forest trail this morning. Is that not enough?

I did feel her nearby last night and again this morning; I still do. But it's not the same as having her here with me physically.

> It could be if you'd allow yourself to be fully open

to that. Listen for the signs. Before you ran, you meditated. And before you meditated, you dedicated your prayer to Emmie Lou. You then opened *A Course in Miracles* to today's passage and found Emmie—and all others—speaking to you.

"I am not a body. I am free," the passage read. Was that not Emmie Lou reassuring you?

Yes. I think it must have been.

And so it was. Walk on now. And as you do, listen for the twittering of birds in the trees overhead and for the rustle of leaves and for the soft, gentle song of breezes that will remind you of your warm little dog who is herself walking beside you along the mountain trails.

She is not a body; she is free.

And so are you all. All beautiful, all free.

Go forth, unafraid. Take the gifts from Emmie Lou, her unbridled exuberance, her joy and devotion, and share these with all the world. You may think she has left you as she ventures forth on her journey of life; but, in fact, she has not. For a little of her remains with you, and a little of you has followed her.

Your journeys are forever entwined by love.

Fifty-Seven

"All things bright and beautiful, All creatures great and small, All things wise and wonderful, The Lord God made them all."
–Cecil Frances Alexander

And then there was Annie. Little Annie. She came to us after and left before Emmie Lou. Emmie loved her, as did we all.

But how strange it all was, God; perhaps you can help us understand.

Annie arrived at our home when she was about five years old, having been abandoned by a family—or the father of the family, anyway, who had little patience and a short fuse. A classic border collie, Annie was high-spirited by nature and a bit naughty at times. We'd actually heard about her long before we adopted her because she'd appeared on the evening news as the dog that had herded a group of the family's horses into a ditch! Wild and crazy and fearless, Annie got into all sorts of trouble.

But she was lovable, too, and very sweet. One of John's colleagues cajoled him into adopting her in an effort to save her from any more of the father's abuse; and at our first meeting,

Annie raised herself up onto her back legs, placed a front paw on each of my shoulders, looked me in the eye and licked my face. We were buddies from that moment on.

Unbeknownst to us, though, Annie had left behind a friend named Danny, a dog whom she had loved since she was a puppy. The two had been inseparable, and Danny was heartbroken when Annie left. Though Annie and Emmie Lou came to love one another, too, Annie never forgot Danny, as we later discovered.

Annie's spirit was beautiful; I always thought she was an 'old soul.' One day, for example, as I drove home from work, I found her sitting in the front yard, surrounded by a multitude of dogs that were gazing up at her with rapt attention. To be honest, the scene reminded me of a painting I'd once seen of Jesus with his disciples. Wherever Annie wandered, the neighboring dogs followed; they adored her. The problem was, Annie led them here, there and everywhere, racing into the street at times with her entourage streaming behind her; and we all worried about that. She took to nipping at people, too, just for fun, until John and I began to fear that someday she'd become a liability beyond which we could handle. Still we loved her.

Six months passed.

One day at lunchtime, John David, unable to find an English paper he'd written for his next class, ran home to retrieve it. Babe, a neighborhood dog, was waiting outside; and Annie, seeing her through the window and spotting John as he unlocked the front door, bolted past him before he could stop her. She raced after Babe into the street just as the mailman rounded the corner in his mail truck and hit her. She died almost instantly.

In the days following her death, Annie appeared in spirit to several of us in odd and inexplicable ways. But the strangest story of all came from John's colleague who had arranged for the adoption in the first place.

"How's Annie?" she demanded the following Monday, five days after Annie's death. She didn't wait for an answer. "She's dead, isn't she?" she continued. "And I'll bet she died on Wednesday, am I right?"

John was taken aback. "How'd you know that?" he asked.

His colleague proceeded to tell him about the phone call she'd received over the weekend from her friend Mary, Annie's former owner who had loved Annie and who had solicited help in finding a new home for her in order to stop the beatings by her husband. This is the story she told:

On the afternoon of Annie's death, Mary had been working in her kitchen when she heard frenzied barking coming from Danny's kennel. Fearing something was wrong with her usually mild-mannered dog, Mary hurried outside to check on him. Upon entering the yard, she smelled the scent of roses and knew in her heart, for some reason I don't understand, that Annie was back—in fact, that something terrible had happened to her and that she had come home to say goodbye.

Drawing nearer to the barking, Mary spied Danny lunging again and again at the kennel door, trying desperately to escape; and nothing she could say or do would calm him. At last, fearing he would hurt himself if he continued, she opened the gate and unlatched the door. In an unusual display of exuberance, Danny bolted, barking ecstatically and racing at top speed after something. Though she called to him to stop, he just kept going. It was the way he'd always acted when Annie was around, she told her friend. His spirit, which had been crushed the day Annie had vanished from his life, had returned; and it was magnificent to watch. But at that very instant, Mary's husband, the man who had abused Annie, drove his pick-up truck around the corner and hit Danny, who died instantly—only hours after Annie herself had passed.

"Mary told me she knew without doubt that Annie had come back to take Danny with her. She asked only that I confirm this with you."

We were heartbroken at losing Annie but awed by the story. Please help us, God, to understand it all.

Annie's charismatic spirit did indeed attract people and other dogs to her (those who were not nipped by her, that is). She was a blessing to you, Pam, but also a risk, and it was only a matter of time before she would have brought trouble to your door. As intelligent as she was handsome, Annie instinctively knew this. She loved her new family and would not for all the world have wished you harm, yet she could not contain her wild and reckless nature. And it was that same spirit, so bold and beautiful, that led her outside that day on a last chase through the neighborhood she'd come to love, ending abruptly under the wheels of the mail truck.

It was time to say goodbye, and Annie did just that in little ways that helped your family with its grief. But she hadn't forgotten the others whom she adored, as well, especially her beloved Danny. And she wasn't willing to leave this world without him. He was, of course, only too happy to oblige.

As for Mary, she's always made use of her intuitive powers, always listened to and acted upon those natural abilities that each of you possess in one way or another but that only a small percentage of you ever really develop. She had only to walk outside to know Annie was there; she'd loved Annie, so much so that she'd been willing to let her go in order to save her life. And Annie had loved her, too, and had come back to say goodbye. Impish as she was, Annie chose her own way of reaping revenge on her former owner, the man who'd hurt her and thus caused her exile from Danny, the same man who inadvertently brought about their reconciliation.

Annie lives on, happy and free and forever entwined with all who have ever loved her. She has not left; she walks beside you even now, you and your family, Mary and others, a guardian angel to you all forevermore.

Fifty-Eight

"A conscious lifetime, therefore, is a treasure beyond value."
-The Seat of the Soul by Gary Zukav

Above all else, I want to feel the happiness that comes from being one with who I really am and with all creation, God. And yet, during these last few days since Emmie Lou died, I've felt so listless and empty, so focused on the past and so fearful of the future that I haven't felt much joy in life. I'd like to change that now. I know with your help I can.

Just being aware is all you need, Pam, just making the conscious choice of being appreciative and open to every moment—to *this* moment—and of choosing jubilation and peace in place of anything else you may be feeling. Now, for instance, you're in a classroom with summer school students who are here only because they have to be, because they failed a class last year. They're busy working on an assignment now, but soon they'll be waiting to hear from you. You can be a passive, unenthusiastic teacher, counting the minutes until the class ends. Or you can connect, smile, make a difference and help each child see who he really is and who she wants to be—*and* discover who you really are and who you want to be, as well.

Like the springtime blossom on a fruit tree, your listlessness will naturally drop away as the fruit replaces it, as you become more and more in union with your authentic Self and as you align your personality with your Soul. Listen to your teachers and guides who are present every moment, hovering, waiting to be of service. Be at peace with yourself and all others. Be aware and in awe of each moment, each person and each opportunity to love. As you do this, you can't help but become more and more present, and a deep, abiding happiness will fill your being.

You're making that choice now. As you do, feel the blessings of prosperity and bliss light up the world and all who dwell in it, including these precious students here with you today.

Let them see that you love them; let them see it in your eyes and in your voice, in your enthusiasm and in your smile. Let them see it in all you do, say, think and feel—and you, too, will know that it is everywhere and in everyone, in your students, in yourself and in all the world, visible and invisible, here in Heaven and here on Earth.

Fifty-Nine

"Destiny is not a matter of chance; it is a matter of choice."
-William Jennings Bryan

It's been a few weeks since we've talked, God, and I've missed you. I've been a bit under the weather, as you know, but tonight I needed to get out for a walk.

The night was beautiful, the sky a starlet canopy, and the snow, soft and light under my feet. Before me, the road stretched out, long and winding, like a white ribbon. It was lovely, yet for some reason I felt a bit sad.

I kept thinking about my life, about all the messes I've made along the way, and kept wishing I could do a better job.

Will I ever learn, God? Or will I go from one relationship to another and from one lifetime to another, repeating the same mistakes? Will I, Father?

Father, will I?

I don't know, Pam. You tell me.... Will you?

Sick and tired...

I've been pretty sick over the last few weeks, so sick, in fact, that I actually stayed home from work a few days, and that's unusual for me. No matter how much I rested, drank fluids and did all the other usual stuff, I felt lousy.

The day before yesterday as I was getting ready to meditate, I opened *A Course in Miracles* and turned to the morning quote. "Let me recognize the problem so it can be solved," it said.

It seemed appropriate.

I've always believed in a mind-body connection. If ever I'm ill—a rare occurrence, I'm happy to say—I try to figure out what might be going on in my life to cause the condition. Sometimes when I've been overly busy, my worn-out body has seemed to say, "Slow down. Rest. Take it easy for a day or two." But this time, it seemed more complicated than that.

All day as I thought about the quote, I listened for inner wisdom and guidance. At last it came, or so I thought.

'I haven't really forgiven John yet,' I realized with surprise, 'and the bitterness of that, the poison I'm unconsciously ingesting, is literally making me sick.'

Yet for several months now, I'd assumed I was finally over him, thought I'd truly forgiven him (if I had anything to forgive) and believed I'd at last moved on with my life. Apparently I hadn't.

'Well,' I thought, 'if I haven't, I'm ready now—more than ready—to be over it, to forgive, and to move on to a happier place.'

Certain I'd discovered the problem and, therefore, the solution, I relaxed, went to bed early and slept soundly. To my surprise, I awoke the next morning to a body that was as achy and ill as it had been the day—the many days—before.

With a cup of tea in hand, I slipped off to my meditation room again, grabbed *A Course in Miracles* and opened to the day's quote. It was similar to the one from the day before. "Let me recognize my problems have been solved," it read. And in that moment, as I sat staring at the words, I understood that my forgiveness of John, or lack thereof, was not the problem, at all—at least, not the real problem. I had no idea what it was, but I felt confident I'd eventually find out.

All day, I rested, pondering the quotes and wondering what, if anything, my body, the Universe, God or my Authentic Self was trying to say. Early in the evening as I sat alone by the fire, it came to me; and in that instant, I knew I'd uncovered the Truth.

'I haven't forgive *myself*,' I thought.

This wasn't about John or anyone else; it was about me. I hadn't forgiven myself—for not being able to keep my marriage together, for making mistakes in my personal and professional life, for being less than perfect as a mother, wife, sister, daughter, teacher and friend, and for anything and everything else I saw as 'wrong' with me.

Pulling out pen and paper, I began to write. Then I cut the sheet up into little strips, each with a statement on it, and knelt before the fire. Taking each piece, I read the words out loud, adding, "I forgive myself for..." and dropped the fragments, one by one, into the fire.

Who would have believed the power of such a simple ritual!

This morning I awoke feeling vibrant and happy again, very much alive and well, very much my Self. I'll likely need to revisit these issues periodically; I'm not so naive as to think they've gone away forever after a lifetime of self-abuse. But I'm stronger now and primed to deal with each as it arises.

I believe that everything—every feeling, every encounter, every relationship and every moment, even the negative ones—have offered me as many gifts over the years as sorrows. I'm grateful for them all. To each, I say thanks. To those that no longer serve me, while releasing them to the Universe for healing and love, I say goodbye. I wish them well.

And I move on...

Sixty

"God is but love and, therefore, so am I."
-A Course in Miracles

Thank you for this peace, God. Already I'm feeling whole again after only a few days since my illness.

"Father, am I ever going to heal?" I asked over and over.

"I don't know. Are you?" You challenged me.

"Father, help me sleep tonight," I prayed.

"Help yourself," You responded. And I did.

Your reminders prompted me to take action, to make decisions, to stop whining and find the peace inside that was there, waiting, all along. By refusing to do the work for me, you empowered me to do it for myself. And yet I felt your support, your compassion, your guides ministering to me all along the way.

You've also helped me to relax, to unclench my fists and to quit clinging to a past that wasn't right for me anymore. You showed me the way to help myself, to let go, to detach. You made me realize that happier times await me but that I don't have to wait for them; I can be happy right now if I choose to be. You taught me to love myself instead of wishing for someone else to love me first.

Thank you.

Thank your Self, Pam, and your guides.

More and more you're looking at this woman—this Pam Carlquist—from the vantage point of an outsider, peering in at her through an open window, noting her passing thoughts, her fears, her obsessions; laughing gently at them and helping her to take herself lightly and to move forward with grace, compassion and love.

As she blesses her brothers, as she praises her sisters, as she forgives herself, so she becomes a savior to the world. One cannot open oneself to love and forgiveness without gaining it not only for oneself but also for everyone else, since giving and receiving are one, in truth. Each time you're able to see through to the beauty that abides in others, you expand the beauty within yourself and shine it forth for all to see.

As you take control of your thoughts, noting the fearful or negative ones and consciously ousting them, replacing them with loving, peaceful ones, you raise your energy levels to love, joy, peace and enlightenment. Most people live their whole lives in the lower energy levels of fear and anxiety. But each has the power to change that; and as even one individual makes that choice, the rippling effect is enormous.

Make that choice now, Pam, if you will. Keep making it, and all the world will profit.

Sixty-One

"Forgiveness is the fragrance that the violet sheds on the heel that has crushed it."
–Mark Twain

This new relationship has brought up some other interesting questions, God. Here's a man who has so many complications in his life—two young boys and an ex-wife who seems out to get all she can from her ex-husband, even to the detriment of the children. As a result, he's so consumed by anger and sorrow and the very act of survival that he has little energy for anything else. I've become his confidante, his sounding board and his friend, which is fine except that I'd grown used to being something more.

And yet, a friend and confidante is no small thing, Pam. You hoped for something more, you say. But I say to you, there is nothing more, for love is all there is. To minister to another with soft, soothing words is as beautiful and intimate as curling up next to another, cheek to cheek, naked breast to naked breast. Each is an expression of love.

Well, maybe. I'm not so sure; we'll see how it goes.

But tell me, God, why do so many divorces lead to such acrimony? Greed, anger and vindictiveness seem to take away all reason and common sense, even among the most intelligent of people. Worst of all, I think, is the eradication of all the good memories, all the happy times each couple shared, since how can they bear to reminisce when their hearts are filled with hatred? It would be like erasing years—for me, more than half my life—if I blocked from my mind the experiences I once shared with John.

And yet this seems to be more common than naught amongst the divorced people I know. This is the real evil side effect, I think, of separation and divorce, not the actual moving apart physically but the emotional bitterness, the Demon and Great Destroyer that adds to the pain, that obscures the joy and that tears people who once loved one another apart forever.

All of life's experiences are but passing fancies that each of you has created in order to heal and evolve. How you respond to each largely determines the degree of your happiness—or unhappiness—in this lifetime. Each marriage, each separation, each birth, each death, each reunion, each divorce holds an opportunity for heartbreak or joy. Not the situation itself, so much as the way you react to it, will ultimately lift you to heaven or cast you into the depths of hell. Either way, you will have created the denouement for yourself, and you will inevitably learn from it and from all experiences in this lifetime or in another. You must. It's the way you are. Your

personality may wail and resist, but your soul seeks
only love; for Love is what you are.

Yes, I guess you're right. (Of course, you're right; you're
GOD, after all!) And you've helped me to come to this point in
my life. At first, I was as hurt and bitter as anyone else when I
realized John had gone for good. I felt betrayed and bruised and
very sad, and my ego was positively screaming with rage. I suspect
it's why so much anger persists after divorce.

My friend is certainly feeling that now. The other day out of
the blue, he asked me this question: If I discovered without doubt
that John had been having an affair during our marriage, would I
ever be able to forgive him?

I answered without hesitation, "I already have," and meant it.
Not that I know or even necessarily suspect that he did. It's just
that I've learned from *A Course in Miracles*, from all of my talks
with you and from my own experiences that I can have no peace
unless I forgive—that is, unless I can see beyond any perceived
offense to the perfection and goodness within us all; in this case,
within John. And I DO!

That's good to hear, Pam. Because it's up to you,
each of you, whether you shrivel up inside or whether
you allow each experience to lead you to a more open
and compassionate state. I'd suggest to all my children
who hold such grievances but who yearn for peace,
that you pray for your former partners and wish them
well, even if you can only utter syllables without
meaning at first. Gradually, as you perpetuate this act
of forgiveness, even in pretense, something inside will
begin to melt, some secret part of you will bud and
blossom; and you will feel the sunshine of your soul

flourish once more.

You are my creations, the children of Light. As you forgive one another, you will discover that which you've been seeking all along. And you'll know that the relationship you thought brought nothing but sorrow has become the instrument of joy and rest.

Live, if you will. I would have you live, my children. I would have you be happy and at peace—but only if you deem that for yourself.

No matter what you choose and no matter when, know that I love you forever.

Sixty-Two

"Just trust yourself; then you will know how to live."
-Johann Wolfgang von Goethe

I've been thinking quite a bit about this most recent relationship, God, and I'm beginning to feel it may not be right for me. I'm disappointed because I do like this man and see so many good qualities in him. AND I had assumed that once I 'fell in love' again, "it would be forever," as the song goes. And maybe it will be, someday. But for now, I'm not so sure.

Last night, for instance, I caught myself judging my new friend (my six-month-old new friend, that is) and finding so many faults with him as I kept hearing him boast—about his sons, himself, his sons, himself, ad nauseam. I just wanted to get away, and I began to look at my life this summer as a complete waste. Too much time invested in a relationship that will likely go nowhere. Too much effort expended on becoming physically fit and attractive to men. Too much energy devoted to trivial things and too much money spent on the material—and all at the expense of my peace of mind, my writing and my discussions with you.

I'm pretty frustrated with it all, as you can see, God. And I'm sorry I've neglected you.

> And yet you've never left me, Pam, for I've been with you through it all—and with the friend you've judged, as well, for always we are one.
>
> Though you may feel that the summer's been wasted, it hasn't been. You're traveling along your journey of life, and your friend is walking beside you. Yes, he has his insecurities; but so do you, lest why would his bother you so much. Bless him, listen to him and help him on his way. Whether this romance will last or not matters not in the least. How you treat this man and all others while you have the opportunity is what counts. As you open your heart to him, as you hold out a steadying hand, you give your heart and hand to all. And you remember who you *really* are.
>
> Yes, you've squandered much time on the physical and material; however, even that's fine so long as you do all with purpose and passion. Abundance, youth, money—all are yours if you choose them to be. But more, so much more, is available to you and all. Always.

Whew! I feel better already, God. I knew I would if I just took the time to talk to you.

It's been interesting, this evolving as a single woman over the last 21 months since John and I separated. More than half my life up until then was spent in marriage, and I always thought that's what I wanted. Now I'm not so sure. I kind of like this single life, now that enough time has passed to give me a little more perspective on it all. Relationships are a bit complicated, and I'm beginning to realize just how much I 'need my space.' In fact, when it comes right down to it, I'm beginning to think I prefer being single and alone—or, at least, alone whenever I feel like being alone.

> You're never alone, Pam, though certainly you're entitled to your 'space,' as you put it. Remember that though moods come and go, relationships are eternal. Therefore, make an effort, if you will, to be your best self with everyone you know; you'll be happier in the long run. Go off by yourself if you must, but be kind always, no matter how you're feeling—*if* you want true peace, that is. Then you'll have no regrets. Love or a call for love, how will you answer?

I'll answer with love, God—or, at least, I'll try. Remind me, please, if I forget.

> Of course, I will if that's what you wish.

I do. Still, I'm glad I've come to the realization that I'm as happy being single as I was being married—happier, in a way, but only because I'm finally dealing with some of the issues that diminished my contentment in the past; it's freeing, to say the least. And you've sustained me in this, so much. Thank you.

Also, this less-than-perfect relationship with my not-so-new friend and, of course, the pain associated with my separation from John have propelled me to this point and have, therefore, been well worth the aggravation. I'm grateful for them because they've inspired me to confront my fears and move past them. It's certainly taken me a while—a lifetime, in fact, maybe many lifetimes and probably many more to follow—and still I have such a long road to walk. But I'm on my way, and I'm enjoying the view!

This latest romance, I'm afraid, was a microcosm of so many others, as I'm sure you know. I felt strong and happy at first, excited to have a special man in my life again but confident with or without him; and I do think when you're feeling good, amazing things happen. Of course, I loved hearing someone tell me I was wonderful. Don't we all? I needed that, or so I thought.

Once his children entered the equation, though, everything changed. As he assumed custody of them for the summer, his focus shifted; it had to, and I understood that. Still, as I became less a priority for him and more a convenience, those insecurities I'd shoved away into some tiny corner of my brain imploded. Boy, oh boy, did they ever! I began worrying every minute about the way I looked and the things I said. I felt shy and awkward, at times, and at a loss for words; and, of course, that just made me seem less attractive to him—and to myself. Thus, the cycle continued.

Yes, I saw your pain, Pam.

I know you did, and you helped me, God. Maybe because of that and because I'd finally begun basing my worth on who I was rather than on what I had or who liked me, the emotional toll was minimal compared to some past relationship meltdowns and especially compared to what I'd just experienced with John. This time, I was stronger and better prepared for what was happening. I knew for sure that what I wanted more than I yearned for this man or for anyone or anything else was peace, the serenity that comes from a deep, abiding wellspring of joy that lies within us all. I was having a dialogue with You, after all, God, and it had changed me, changed the very makeup—or, at least, my awareness—of my cells, my essence, my eternality, my self worth and my vulnerability that was ultimately invulnerable. I had a knowing, even in the midst of my pain and despair, that I would be fine, more than fine, that I was grounded enough and steady enough as long as I kept hold of your hand to walk through this—or any other—fire and to come out whole.

And so, God, while a part of me, the small part, was bemoaning the fact that this intimate and 'perfect' relationship was changing, another part, the bigger, better one, was—IS—watching and mulling it over and talking to me the way you've done during our conversations over the last year.

"Are you really going to do this again?" it asks. "Aren't you tired of the pain?"

"I can't help it," I snap. "It's the way I am."

"If you say so," it acquiesces then adds, "These are only thoughts, Pam, your thoughts, the ones you created. You can change them any time."

"Oh." I ponder this a while. "I guess I can. I forgot."

"Well, forget no more," it or maybe you, God, maybe both of us, answer.

And so I do. I stop being insecure, with defiance. I purposely dress with a casualness that defies criticism, act with a nonchalance that dismisses judgment and say whatever comes into my head, just so long as it isn't unkind. I am myself so much that I almost don't recognize me—and neither does my friend, who suddenly seems interested again. But it's too late.

Sometimes I forget, and my uncertainties leap at the open door. But pretty soon that other part of me wakes up from its brief snooze and stands in the doorway, glowering.

"Do you want to be happy or not?" it asks.

I nod sheepishly.

"Then get rid of those." It glances toward my unruly guests, and I remember suddenly who I am and who I forever want to be—me, the authentic Me. And what I want to have far more than any silly relationship that reeks of unhealthy codependency or one-sidedness or anything else that doesn't feel good.

And I notice that now that I love myself a little more, I don't care so much whether or not my not-so-new friend or anyone else loves me back.

It's nice. It feels good. I like it.

Sixty-Three

"I'm ready, willing and able to accept more good than I have ever experienced, imagined, manifested, or expressed before."
-Dr. Michael Beckwith

After much hemming and hawing, it's finally over, God. This relationship isn't working for either of us, so it's time I gather up my courage and say goodbye. The trouble is, as I discovered after John left, 'goodbye' is a very hard thing for me to say. It always has been; I just didn't realize *why* until now.

This morning I read an article that helped me make sense of this. According to several studies, when a child loses someone close to her through death or abandonment, she often has more difficulty than most when faced with future separations or loss, even the death of an acquaintance. Each new goodbye carries with it the remembrance of the past.

With my parents' deaths, I learned early on that goodbye is sometimes a forever thing. That trauma has lingered so that whenever an important relationship, particularly a romance, ends, it feels like death to me. Maybe it's why I've remained friends, or tried to, with so many past partners and with John. Besides not wishing to harbor bad feelings, I wanted to avoid their 'deaths.'

As I've contemplated the ending of this latest affair, many of the fears that cropped up after John and I separated, albeit to a lesser degree, have come back. I've felt that same hollow pit in my stomach, that dull, constant hum of anxiety and that awful sense of low self-worth. I've wondered what was wrong with me, and I've known a deep and abiding sorrow for this loss.

The other day, I sat, phone in hand, ready to call this man and say goodbye, but I just couldn't do it. I hadn't even said the words, and I was already grieving for him as though he were dead.

Intellectually, I know death is a natural part of life, a transition to a new form or way of being. I know change is inevitable and good more times than not; and I realize no one can really separate since we're all one.

I've heard you, God, and I've listened, and I think I really understand all of that intellectually. And yet...

...I still have a very hard time saying goodbye.

I also know I need to deal with this now; otherwise, I'll keep hearing that 'baby' on my doorstep—more and more babies and more and more wailing and crying to be free. It's time now to forever release the unhappy habit of holding on when everything inside is telling me to let go. Today I'm ready to move forward, and so I must.

This is an opportunity to see goodbye as a natural and inevitable part of hello.

Yes, today. Now...

Goodbye, my friend. Goodbye, John. Goodbye, past. Goodbye, pain.

Hello, Pam. Hello, God.

Hello! Oh, hello!

Sixty-Four

"And the day came when the risk to remain tight in a bud was more painful than the risk it took to blossom."
-Anais Nin

Hello to you, my daughter. Hello.

I'm feeling a little like you did the day your son John picked up the phone and called his former girlfriend to invite her to prom. All his young life, you and your husband had led him by the hand along this road to kindness and joy. But at last he was ready to walk that path alone.

You've begun your trek to freedom, as well; and you're racing, my dear, up that winding and solitary trail on your own strong legs.

No, life has not worked out for you as planned. You're not in a successful marriage at the moment, but you're a good person nonetheless and content with your lot. Yes, you've made mistakes along the way—as a wife, a mother, a teacher and a friend. But you've changed some of your students' and loved one's lives in most positive ways, as well; they've told you so on many occasions, and people who have known them have, too. And you've been a wonderful mom. Ask your sons; they love you so.

And, no, you aren't in a romantic relationship with your former partner any more. But that's fine, isn't it? You were patient and kind and very loving; so was he. It just didn't last for a variety of reasons. That doesn't make the collaboration a failure or a waste of time. You each brought healing to the other and to yourselves. Now, as friends, you can offer one another a different kind of balm. Be happy that it has worked out as it has.

Nothing in your life or any other has ever really gone wrong. All is as it should be. Each change, each challenge, each supposed ending has offered you and all the opportunity to evolve and become more loving and compassionate beings. Without some of these setbacks, you'd probably not have come as far in this lifetime as you have. Your intentions to move past fear to energy levels of joy and peace have emerged from the pain you've faced.

You co-created this life, Pam, as a means of healing, of remembering your true Self and of paying your karmic debts—not because you have to, mind you, but because you've elected to as you seek eternal peace and unity with me and with all. You could have remained in the Spirit Realm, but instead you chose this life in this body as this self, this Pam. A frail little girl you were but spunky, too, and full of vibrant energy. You laughed and cried easily as the doted-upon baby of your family and played that role to the hilt. But even then you were full of fears, for you'd brought those with you to this lifetime. You came to learn and grow, to evolve into your true and pure Self, to align your personality as this girl Pam with your Soul.

You've faced many problems, but you've had so many happy times, as well. Always, always, though, fear has hovered about you. Will life always be this way, you've wondered during moments of bliss, or will it vanish and leave me lonely and alone? Many of your fears seem to have come true, have they not? And yet you've plodded on, weary and bruised to the bone, yet determined to seek and find peace, joy, light and love during this lifetime. And find it you will—you *are*—as you but choose to let it be.

Take care of this Pam, this daughter, this child. Treat her with tenderness and love. She deserves that. Observe her thoughts, and help her repel all fearful ones; help her wage war on them—nay, help her find peace. She does not merit such a meager, fearful life. She tries so hard. Bless her. Forgive her. Love her. As you do, so she will bless, love and forgive her Self and others, too.

She'll need some prompting. Remind her. For then, how beautiful her time on earth will be.

Sixty-Five

"The great lesson from the true mystics... is that the sacred is in the ordinary, that it is to be found in one's daily life, in one's neighbors, friends, and family, in one's back yard."
-Abraham Maslow

Another holiday season has come and gone, God. It could have been quite lethal, especially in view of my recent breakup; and I will admit to a little sadness along the way.

But for the most part, it's been filled with merriment and laughter, friends and family, love and peace. Thanks to you and all of your kind words over the last year, I was able to make some choices that have helped.

I've begun every day of this holiday break with prayer and meditation, the perfect reminder of who I am and how precious each day is. My readings, directed by you, I believe, have also helped me replace lingering fears with peace. Thank you.

Then I've headed outdoors for a run with Ebony or a snowshoe outing or a cross-country ski or a walk. I've seen the depths of your beauty in the snow-flecked sky, the wintry fields, the wind-rocked trees; and it has touched my soul, reminding me of the beauty of all creation. Thank you for this.

I've called friends and loved ones every day, those I see often and those I don't. I've heard the surprise in their voices and felt their joy, which has warmed my heart and made me cherish all who have touched my life, those who've been my harshest critics and those who've been my greatest support—teachers and guides, all of them, who have helped me see more clearly.

I've challenged myself on the ski hill nearly every afternoon, defying gravity, floating through powder, cruising down mogul-filled runs. And I've known the exhilaration of being alive and the wonder of flight. You've skied with me, God—I've felt you on every turn—and we've laughed out loud. Thank you for being my friend.

Each night, I've partied with confidantes and neighbors, viewed uplifting films and listened to concerts. I've sat by the fire with my sons, enjoyed candlelight dinners and taken starlit walks with little Ebony, who rolls in the snow and barks and reminds me of how joyful a world at peace is if we embrace it in our hearts.

And yesterday, on Christmas, I spent a nearly perfect day. First, a call and a gift from my once-boyfriend-now-friend; then a day with John and the boys—opening presents by the fire, sitting down to Christmas breakfast, skiing together on powdery slopes, laughing, rubbing backs and sharing dinner with family and friends. How lovely it all was! How warm and happy. A perfect Christmas day!

I don't know what the future holds for John and me or anyone else. At the end of the evening, we went our separate ways, and my heart ached a little—but only a little, for you whispered to me; and I chose once again a snowy walk and a decision to be happy, no matter what, to count my blessings not my losses. For there is no loss, only love. You've taught me that and imbued me with this sense of joy and peace.

Thanks for all your reminders, God.

Whenever I stumble, as I often do, you pick me up, brush me off and send me on my way again. Thanks for not carrying me too far, for letting me develop the blisters and calluses that will make each bend in the road all the sweeter.

Life is magical, and I'm savoring the journey.

I love you, God, my dear, dear Friend. Thank you for everything.

You've said it all, my child. Keep saying it. Say it over and over—"I love you," "I love you," "I love you"—to all you meet, to all of life's experiences, to yourself, to Me, to all Creation.

I love you...

I love you...

I love you...

The way it is...

I slept well again last night, and that always helps. Today I feel rested and whole. But not just today, I'm realizing...

Lately, I've begun to accept and even value the situation between John and me, realizing we'll never be together again in the way we were. I think I'll always love him, but maybe I can begin loving him more and more as a friend or even as a brother. He's been good to me in so many ways, and I'll always be grateful for that. I've been good to him, too. We've had our moments of ego and unkindness but, overall, the joys have far outweighed the sorrows. I'm glad of that.

Sometimes now, right in the middle of whatever I'm doing, even when I'm stewing about what might have been or worrying about what might happen next, I stop suddenly and a light goes on—a bright, brilliant burst of light that pulses in and spreads its warmth right through me—and I see (I actually, literally SEE) the extraordinarily wonderful life I'm living RIGHT NOW, JUST AS IT IS. And I realize I'm fine just as I am, on my own. I'm more than fine; I'm happy.

Don't get me wrong, I'm sad, too, at times—a deep, biting, sock-in-the-stomach kind of sadness that wishes so much I could have rescued our marriage and our lives together. But even deeper, buried within my soul, I feel a kind of grace, a gentle forgiveness, for myself and John, for the two of us not knowing how and not being able to make our marriage last. And with that gentleness comes a kind of joy that seems to emanate from my very being.

It's hard to explain, but I have a knowing, a wellspring of 'all's-right-with-my-world' that lights up my heart and soul.

It's a weird sensation, the sadness-so-deep-you-can't-breathe-at-times and yet the gladness-so-warm-and-glowing-you-can't-thank-God-enough that live side by side inside of me. It's a new feeling, or a new combination of feelings, and it comes often enough now that I know I'm going to be all right. I'm going to move past the pain and live again, really LIVE. And I'm pretty excited about that; I'm looking forward to discovering just what my new life will be.

Actually, I already see it. I'm moving toward it RIGHT NOW. No more waiting! This is what IS, and I'm grateful for it, all of it, even the sorrowful parts. Maybe if I'd been more grateful when John and I were together, we'd still be together—or maybe not. It doesn't matter; that's the wonderful thing. Only NOW matters, every beautiful, magical, sad, happy, kind, cruel, all-that-ever-is NOW. And I'm thrilled about that, open and eager and itching to see, moment by moment, just exactly what Now is.

Sixty-Six

I feel these discussions together are almost over, God, yet I don't want them to end. They've brought me so much comfort and peace over the last year.

We can talk whenever you wish, Pam. We have so much to discuss. Another time, perhaps?

Yes, please. I'd like that.

You've been such a good friend to me, God. So many people believe in an impersonal god who doesn't really care. And yet, you care. How did I get so lucky to be able to talk to you like this? I feel as though you're my best friend—next to Ebony, that is (just kidding, God, sort of)—and that I can do anything, say anything, be anything, tell you anything; and you'll still love me.

Of course, I will and do and always shall—love you and all of my creations, my dearest, most blessed, most precious beings of light and peace. And you ARE, you know, you ARE, whether you feel the joy of it every moment or not, and even if you *never* feel it during this lifetime—still you are all my beloved children. Your souls realize this, even if your personalities during this lifetime don't. Ultimately each of you will come to know this; you must, for you are the offspring of Love—nay, more, you are Love Itself.

I do know it. I forget sometimes, but it's always there in the very core of my being; and it makes me glad. And yet, God, there are so many on this earth who don't even care about you. How do you connect with them?

Any way they wish, Pam. Any way, at all.

You created this relationship with me, or co-created it; and anyone else can, too, each in the form that works best for that individual—even if that means not knowing or believing in me, at all. The discourse you and I have engaged in over the last year might have been very different—stilted and formal and clothed in any rhetoric, traditional or otherwise, that you chose. Instead, you spoke to me as an intimate friend, and I responded as such.

I've given you and all my precious creations free volition in every aspect of life. This discussion with me was born of your free will. Your conversing with me like this—joking at times, crying out for help, asking questions, cursing me and your fate—made our alliance all the more authentic because it is OUR connection, Pam, unique and personal to the two of us. It doesn't diminish your reverence for me, and it doesn't lessen—or bolster—my love for any other. I *am* Love. And so are you, each of you, Love. Any one of you can create anything you want at any time and in any way, even the very relationship you foster—or deny—with your God and source. Friend, father, ruler, despot, judge, king—I'm called by so many names. Out of gentleness, I honor them all. But ultimately I know only one, and that name is Love.

You *are* Love, God. Thank you for being my friend.

Thank you, Pam. And thanks to all my children everywhere, even those who don't know me.

This is a new age for each of you, a new dawn, a new opportunity for life with all of its shadows and songs. What will this millisecond hold for each of you—and this one, and this? Only you can decide; only you can make the distinction between love and fear. Choose love, if you will. Choose peace, if you wish. Choose me, if you would. No matter, I choose you all.

It's a new now, a new day, a new instant in Eternity. What will you make of it? Who will you be? Remember, it's your...

We know, God—it's our...

...yes, our...

...choice always.

Always.
Are you ready at last to move on, my children, to
love and peace today?

I am, God. I can only speak for myself, but I'm ready, right
now.

Good. That's a start.
Let's begin...

10 years later...

Ten years! Can it really be 10 years?

On the one hand, it feels like another lifetime now and I, another person. On the other, it all comes back as I reread the pages as though it were yesterday. But it's not—"It's today, my favorite day," as Piglet from *Winnie the Pooh* would say. And it *is*.

So much has changed since then. So much has shifted.

In one of our earliest discussions, God said to me, "Trust that all will work out as it should and that it will be beautiful, far beyond anything either of you thought possible." He was right. But then, maybe I shouldn't be so surprised by that!

My life—and, I think, John's, too—is beautiful, beyond anything we expected. I'm retired from the public schools but still teach literature and writing courses part-time at a university. I travel fairly often, with my most recent trips including a trek, river rafting adventure and jungle safari in Nepal, a vacation to Hawaii, a visit with my son and his girlfriend in Canada, a whirlwind tour of New York City, a hike into the depths of the Grand Canyon and two 10-day 10-hour-a-day silent meditation retreats just outside of Yosemite and Sun Valley, respectively. I still run, hike, bike, ski, garden, write and dance. I've been fortunate in my 'love life' and have had several wonderful partners along the way, all who have added—and still add—joy and goodness to my life.

Like Mama, I've tried on many different outfits over the last 10 years, looking for the ones that fit best; and like my friend Janine, whose sweetheart was killed in a motorcycle accident, I've held my finger over the font of joy once or twice too often—fearful, I suppose, that the wellspring would run out. I try not to do that anymore.

John and I, though divorced now, are still good friends. I take care of his dogs while he works, and he takes care of mine when I go out of town or just need help. We made a commitment a long time ago to be kind to one another and to make the divorce a win-win situation. Since we'd both worked hard all our lives, we wanted to come out of this ahead; and we did. I'll always remember one incident during a difficult part of the divorce proceedings when the mediator turned to me and asked, "Are you sure you can afford to keep that house on a teacher's salary?" To which John replied, "I'll do whatever it takes so she can." And he did. I still live in my dream home today.

I've helped John, too. Several years ago, during the remodeling of his own house, John developed a health condition that required major surgery. Upon his discharge from the hospital, I invited him and his then significant other to spend a few weeks in my guest room while he recuperated, free from paint fumes and all the other major remodeling hazards. It went well. Then the following summer, John volunteered to help me replace a large deck at the front of my house. For several months, he, my sons and a dear friend and companion spent long hours demolishing the old deck and replacing it with a beautiful new one. We still celebrate birthdays, holidays and other occasions together with our sons and partners. As a result, John David and Will still have a solid, loving family. And so do we all!

I'm happy now, happier, I think, than I've ever been. I'm leading the life I've chosen, doing the things I love and being, for the most part, the person I want to be. I still, of course, have much to learn, do and become, but I'm excited about that. Today *is* my favorite day, and now *is* my favorite time, almost always!

And so it is…

There you are. I wondered where you were, God. You just had to get the last word in, didn't you?

> And the Word was with God, and the Word was God.

Amen to that, God.

Ha!
Amen indeed.

Acknowledgements

To my sons John and Will who remind me of my blessings every day by their very existence, devotion and support, thank you for adding joy and meaning to my life. To my former husband and friend John who continues to be an important presence in my life, thanks for the memories, past, present and future. To my family and friends, partners, pets, students and loved ones, to all who have crossed my path, directly or indirectly, I thank you. Each of you has helped me realize the Oneness, Eternality and Beauty that is forever a part of Life and of us All. To my waggly pups and furry friends Ebony and Zumi who make me run, laugh and play outside in the snow even when I don't want to, thanks for being the perfect examples of love. And to the Source of all that appears in this book and all that exists throughout the Universe, thank you for my life and for the lives and goodness of all beings everywhere.

Bibliography

A Course in Miracles. 2nd Edition. Glen Ellen: Foundation for Inner Peace, 1992.

Beck, Martha. "How to Deal With Major Life Changes." *O Magazine.* Jan. 2004.

Coffin, William Sloane. *Credo.* Louisville: Westminster John Knox Press, 2004.

"Daily Guides." *Science of Mind.* http://www.scienceofmind.com/.

Edited by A. J. Russell. *God Calling.* New York: Russell Dodd, Mead, 1945.

Ehrmann, Max. "Desiderata."1927. http://www.desiderata.com/.

Frost, Robert. "Stopping by Woods on a Snowy Evening" from *The Poetry of Robert Frost*, edited by Edward Connery Lathem. Copyright 1923, © 1969 by Henry Holt and Company, Inc., renewed 1951, by Robert Frost.

Holmes, Ernest. *The Science of Mind.* New York: Dodd, Mead, 1938. Print.

Millman, Dan. *The Way of the Peaceful Warrior.* Tiburon: H.J. Kramer, Inc., 1984.

Mountain Dreamer, Oriah. *The Invitation.* San Francisco: Harper SanFrancisco, 1999.

Peale, Norman Vincent. *The Power of Positive Thinking.* New York: Fireside/Simon & Schuster, 2003.

Rilke, Rainier Marie. *Letters to a Young Poet.* Novato, AC: New World Library, 2000.

Ruiz, Don Miguel. *The Four Agreements: a practical guide to personal freedom.* San Rafael: Amber-Allen Publishing, 1997.

The Holy Bible: King James Version. Minneapolis, MN: World Wide Publications, 1976.

Weiss, Brian. *Many Lives, Many Masters.* New York: Simon and Schuster, 1988.

Zukav, Gary. *The Seat of the Soul.* New York: Simon and Schuster, 1989.

Pam Carlquist is a contemporary author, presenter, life coach and motivational speaker. She also teaches writing and literature courses through the Osher Institute at the University of Utah and travels extensively, sharing the messages of this book with others.

Visit Pam at www.pamelacarlquist.com

Write to her at:

P.O. Box 682825
Park City, UT 84068

Email:
wagglypuppress@gmail.com